AMERICAN
PRO

THE TRUE STORY OF BIKE RACING IN AMERICA

AMERICAN PRO

★ ★ ★ ★ ★ ★ ★

JAMIE SMITH

VELO
press

Boulder, Colorado

3002 Sterling Circle, Suite 100
Boulder, CO 80301–2338 USA

VeloPress is the leading publisher of books on endurance sports. Focused on cycling, triathlon, running, swimming, and nutrition/diet, VeloPress books help athletes achieve their goals of going faster and farther. Preview books and contact us at velopress.com.

Distributed in the United States and Canada by Ingram Publisher Services

Library of Congress Cataloging-in-Publication Data
Name: Smith, Jamie, (Cyclist)
Title: American pro: the true story of bike racing in America / Jamie Smith.
Description: Boulder, Colorado: VeloPress, [2018] |
Identifiers: LCCN 2018012648 (print) | LCCN 2018013090 (ebook) |
   ISBN 9781948006057 (ebook) | ISBN 9781937715762 (pbk.).
Subjects: LCSH: Bicycle racing—United States—History.
Classification: LCC GV1049 (ebook) | LCC GV1049 .S648 2018 (print) |
   DDC 796.6/20973—dc23
LC record available at https://lccn.loc.gov/2018012648

This paper meets the requirements of ANSI/NISO Z39.48-1992
(Permanence of Paper).

Art direction by Vicki Hopewell
Cover design by Kevin Roberson
Cover photo by Jamie Smith
Author photo by Oran Kelly

18 19 20 / 10 9 8 7 6 5 4 3 2 1

For Matthew and Josh Curin and Wyatt, Eden, and Otto Frey.
May you inherit your fathers' passion and energy.

CONTENTS

Preface ix

1 Dreaming Big 1

2 Anatomy of a Niche Sport 13

3 The Road to the Major Leagues 23

4 Cycling's Sponsorship Conundrum 31

5 Some Assembly Required 41

6 Season 1: Pink, Blue, and White 51

7 Partnerships, Mergers, and Acquisitions 65

8 Sophomore Year 71

9 Season 2: Pink and Gray 79

10 Orchestrating a Bike Race 89

11 The Weight of a Pro License 103

12 Season 3: Pink, Gray, and White 109

13 The Friends and Family Plan 125

14 Finding the Right Formula 137

15 Season 4: The Red Army Marches On 147

16 Cycling's Clear and Present Danger 169

17 Uncertainty Sets In 175

18 Season 5: Red and Black 181

19 Closing Up Shop 195

20 The Taking of Fuzhou 201

Epilogue 211

About the Author 217

PREFACE

In a nondescript parking lot in downtown Boston, under the glow of streetlights, volunteers dismantled a bike race course on Congress Street and five teammates packed up their belongings, shook hands, and said their goodbyes.

The 2016 TD Bank Mayor's Cup was the last public appearance of the Astellas Pro Cycling Team. Seven months earlier, their title sponsor had pulled the plug, leaving the team with no contracts for the following season. The next time these riders met, they would be wearing new kits and racing for different teams.

It might be the case that even the most dedicated cycling fans have never heard of the Astellas Pro Cycling Team. Despite being licensed as a professional team, this small Chicago-based team didn't play a memorable role on cycling's world stage.

This is their story, as it played out in the lower ranks of professional bike racing in America. It's nothing short of amazing that two bike-racing fans with a little gumption could start a team at the regional amateur level and then take it from dominating the local race scene to becoming a professional team registered with the Union Cycliste

Internationale (UCI) that competed, and won, internationally. And they did it all with a skeleton crew on a shoestring budget.

I was fortunate to have been involved with the Astellas team in various capacities for most of its five-year run, first as a video producer creating short clips for the American Society of Clinical Oncology (ASCO) trade show, and later as a still photographer documenting their bigger adventures for use on social media. In the end, as a soigneur-like assistant, I performed those menial tasks that fall to anyone willing to do them: handing up water bottles in the feed zone, driving the team van across the country, fetching riders from the airport, and so on. I fell far short of being a true soigneur, but I was all Astellas could afford.

I met up with the team at various events around the country and did my best to help. When not traveling with the team, I followed the livestreams of the bike races and cryptic texts from other teammates who were watching the team race: "Ryan in break. 30 secs to pack. I think they'll stay away." I watched the team grow and mature from my privileged vantage point. Having known the team managers for many years, I had a front-row seat for their struggle to launch a team.

I am a longtime fan of cycling. Since 1986, I've worked in various capacities in the sport that have allowed me to peek behind the curtain to see how it all works. I've been a TV producer, a race promoter, and even a course marshal. I've driven a motorcycle carrying spare wheels. I've been a race announcer at every kind of cycling event imaginable. I was hired as the main announcer at races throughout the 1990s and transitioned to the mobile announcing role at the major American stage races (Amgen Tour of California, the old Tour de Georgia, and the Larry H. Miller Tour of Utah), where I got the unique opportunity to speak to every single spectator along every mile of the course. And throughout all of these experiences, I have remained a license-holding bike racer. I assumed all this would make me some sort of expert on the sport, but I was wrong. It was the time I spent working with the

Astellas Pro Cycling Team that gave me a much deeper understanding of how the sport really works.

Forty-one riders wore the Astellas kit at various times during the team's run, and those riders poured their hearts and their souls into the sport for as long as they were able. *American Pro* is my attempt to put them in the spotlight, if only for a moment.

More than anything, I wanted to show bike-racing fans what's behind the curtain. It's not always what it seems.

CHAPTER 1

DREAMING BIG

Professional bike racing is an amazing sport with loyal fans who happily stand along a remote section of road for hours waiting for a glimpse of their heroes. They'll dress up in ridiculous costumes and hike up a mountainside to cheer on someone they hardly know. After their favorite rider passes by in a whoosh, they'll wait another 20 minutes for the last rider to trundle up the hill. The costumed fan will scream a litany of positive encouragements to the first and last riders and everyone in between, truly believing that it has an effect on the rider's ability to make it to the finish. And it may.

These fans wear their hearts on their sleeves. Their workspaces are adorned with the trinkets recovered from bike races: race posters snagged from the cafe window, routing signs off telephone poles, and stickers from the team cars. The water bottle that Brent Bookwalter discarded onto the side of the road is treated like the Great Chalice of Antioch. Of course it never held a drop of wine, but it once held some of the best hydration mix that Skratch Labs has to offer.

Every spring at the Amgen Tour of California, legions of fans wait for the team buses to pull into town with cameras and felt-tip markers in hand to meet their favorite riders. They come from all across the country to see cycling's version of LeBron James and Ricky Fowler, to actually reach out and touch the riders they've watched on TV racing in the Tour de France. The true aficionados know precisely what time to arrive and precisely where to stand so that they'll be positioned in front of the door when the team bus is finally parked.

The teams that ride in the Amgen Tour of California and the Tour de France are the major leagues, the crème de la crème. They are, in a cycling fan's mind, every bit as famous and wonderful as the New York Yankees. But teams like Astellas are not part of this scene.

The Astellas Pro Cycling Team raced at a level of pro cycling more on par with the Trenton Thunder, the New York Yankees' double-A farm team made up of promising young players who were paid a pittance while gaining valuable experience that they hoped would carry them up to the major leagues.

Despite racing at the lower level of the sport, the Astellas team had their own corps of dedicated followers who tracked their progress throughout the season and made pilgrimages to see them race. Granted, their pilgrimages were likely across a county instead of an entire country. They may not have dressed in costume, but they made poster-board signs and rang cowbells at the bike races. And they knew where the team parked its van each year for, say, the Clarendon Cup in Virginia, and would stop by to say hello before the race.

Over five seasons the Astellas team developed a loyal fan base, and the team earned key victories in popular American races thanks to their willingness to race hard against much tougher opponents. It took five years of bike racing to reach their zenith at the bottom rung of cycling.

It began years before as a daydream.

BIKE RACERS OF ALL LEVELS and abilities think about some strange things when they're on a training ride, including the fantasy of owning a pro team. They let all of their best ideas play out as if $10 million landed in their laps and they could choose the riders and design everything from the ground up.

Sure, it's a fun mental exercise to help fill the hours on a long ride, but the idea of actually starting a professional bike racing team is daunting enough to keep it safely within dreamland. The wherewithal and the shear amount of work it takes to acquire sponsors, organize logistics, and manage a group of athletes is a dream killer.

But that didn't deter Matt Curin.

Matt Curin is your typical bike racer, bike-racing fan, and dreamer. He dreamed the dream and began to mull over all the decisions involved in managing a competitive team while watching the Tour de France. It was years in the making, but Curin eventually set his dream into action.

Curin's racing career began in 1989 as a 15-year-old racer in a local club, the Cadieux Bicycle Club in Detroit. He had as much enthusiasm and ability as everyone else, but not enough raw talent to have a shot at becoming a pro cyclist himself. He raced a lot, spending his summer traipsing across the Midwest with his teammates in search of the next bike-race high that came with winning $30. He learned how bike racing worked and how it didn't. Even as a teen, he picked up on the exasperating and frustrating aspects of the sport that kept it from becoming as mainstream as baseball and football. He readily accepted the idiosyncrasies, as most cyclists do, as he took the unofficial oath of a USA Cycling licensed member: "It is by no means a perfect sport, but it's a damn cool sport regardless, and I love racing my bike, so, flaws be damned, I'm a bike racer for life."

It's not a well-worded or inspirational oath, come to think of it. But it's binding.

Matt Curin is the kind of person that cycling fans would want undertaking a project that helps the sport grow. One of the most polite people walking the Earth, he maintains a deferential demeanor, often self-effacing. Even on issues he knows well, he speaks in a nervous rush as if to get out of the way of the next speaker. He hasn't a mean-spirited bone in his body. And he truly loves the sport of bike racing.

Lacking the skills to garner a pro contract, Curin attended the University of Michigan College of Pharmacy and took the path that diverged from that of a pro cyclist—one leading to a comfortable bed, a full refrigerator, a car that starts, six fully functional bikes in the garage, a wife and kids, medical benefits, a dental plan, and a steady paycheck. In his sophomore year, he took over the presidency of the University of Michigan cycling team in an elaborate procedure that involved raising his hand and expressing interest. At that point in time, the club was at a low organizational ebb and in desperate need of leadership.

Under Curin, the team grew from eight riders in the first year to almost 20 in his senior year due to his enthusiastic recruiting efforts. The team represented the Wolverines at National Collegiate Cycling Association (NCCA) events throughout the Midwest and attended collegiate nationals for the first time in the program's history. Despite the minuscule funding typical of club-level activities, Curin left the Michigan cycling scene better than he had found it, and the experience he gained by chasing funding across the campus proved helpful later on. He made a promise to himself that, were he ever in a position to funnel money into the sport, he would do whatever he could to make it happen.

Two years out of college, after filling prescriptions at small pharmacies, he began working at Pharmacia, a Swedish-American pharmaceutical company. Once established in his role at the Pharmacia offices in Kalamazoo, Michigan, he took his first steps through the looking glass in an attempt to push his dream into reality. He sent emails to anyone in the organization with "marketing" in their title asking them for money to fund a cycling team. He stopped short of begging, but he didn't stop asking until he finally found someone willing to earmark $15,000 from the public relations budget—enough to fund a five-person team consisting of four men and one woman who raced as amateurs throughout the Midwest.

Pharmacia's first team carried the name "Detrol LA Cycling Team" to promote a drug that treated the symptoms of urinary incontinence. Granted, it was not a romantic name for a cycling team but was exactly what one might expect a pharmaceutical company to select. The money from Pharmacia was not necessarily granted to the team with a marketing strategy in mind. It's probably more accurate to say that the money was burped out of an overstuffed budget.

Curin had every intention of helping his company as much as his team. He was off and running.

Detrol LA Cycling was somewhat invisible in the peloton with only two riders who could finish in the lead group of any given Category I/II race, usually around 11th place. Every now and then, they would find themselves on the podium of a regional race, placing among the top three finishers who are invited to appear at the awards ceremony, an accomplishment in any bike race. But with a national sponsor emblazoned across the front, sides, and back of their jerseys, they fooled competitors into thinking the team was a force to be reckoned with.

When a cycling kit is imprinted with the logo of a local bike shop (or chiropractor's office, or engineering firm, etc.), bike racers assume that the rider doesn't pose a big threat. Even if they aren't familiar with the bike shop, their assumption remains unchanged, and nine times out of ten it will be fairly accurate. But when a bike racer sees a national sponsor taking up most of the room on an opponent's kit, they'll do a double take. Even at the amateur level, national-level sponsors usually indicate—rightly or wrongly—a big budget and strong riders. Even if there are only two riders wearing the kit in a race, other racers will draw the conclusion that there exists somewhere a complete team of highly trained and well-supported riders, and that the rest of those riders must be racing elsewhere this particular weekend . . . thank goodness.

But that is not always true. The notoriety of a sponsor does not directly predict the caliber of the team.

Though they garnered only a handful of results, Detrol LA's riders were able to race a full schedule of races they might otherwise have missed. They traveled out of the peninsular Michigan cycling scene, and they represented a professional company as professionally as possible. For Curin, it was a great first effort and the "proof of concept" needed to initiate a second season.

In the second year, the budget grew to $60,000, considered by many to be massive for an amateur team. The team's name changed to the much sexier sounding Pharmacia Cycling Team. The roster grew to eight riders, including some rolleurs who would eventually turn pro. Canadian Jacob Erker rode with Symmetrics and Kelly Benefits Strategies later in his career. Ben Sharp was the reigning national criterium champion and later became a US National Team coach. Adam Watts, former national champion Dave Wenger, and Ohioan Andrew Frey rounded out the roster. Frey had a dual role as rider-manager, handling logistics and spending the boatloads of cash handed down by the sponsor.

The team jelled quickly and developed a one-for-all, all-for-one attitude that helped them get results even against stiff competition. On the very tough Oak Glen stage of the Redlands Cycling Classic in California, without hesitation, Ben Sharp gave his bike to Jacob Erker, who had suffered a mechanical failure that threatened to cause Erker to lose time on the final climb. That and other unselfish moves helped them finish as the top amateur team at that event, a huge result for a new team.

Giddy with the success at Redlands, Matt Curin started to dream of shrink-wrapped team cars, matching warm-up suits, and air travel. But the dream vaporized less than a month later.

Pharmacia had agreed to make four payments over the course of the season totaling $60,000. The first check arrived, and the team was virtually swimming in money. They didn't have time to count it. By the time they arrived in Georgia for the Athens Twilight Criterium in mid-April, Pharmacia had been gobbled up by corporate giant Pfizer, for whom cycling was not a priority. Pfizer promptly cut all funding to the cycling project, leaving Curin in the awkward position of having to hastily call a team meeting in the parking lot of the Atlanta Marriott, where he apologized profusely to the riders, dismantled the team, and put his dream back on the shelf.

Curin soon left the company to join another pharmaceutical company in Indianapolis: Lilly. His move had nothing to do with Pfizer's pulling the funding; it was purely coincidental.

The consolation was that he had actually done it, even if on a very small scale. Curin's modest success at managing a cycling team only fanned the flames further. Sure, he had made some mistakes along the way, but he embraced it as a learning experience.

Curin was just a regular guy. He didn't wear a superhero's cape, and thanks to his rigorous work as a pill researcher, he no longer had the time to maintain a superfit body. He looked the way you'd expect a pharmacist to look: normal. He didn't possess a one of a-kind set of management or organizational skills. The only thing that distinguished him from anyone then, and still today, was moxie. He had the unmitigated gall to ask his employers for money.

And, with the exception of Pfizer, they all said yes.

After a year spent getting to know the lay of the land at Lilly, he tried again and was able to procure a budget of $60,000 by using the "ask everyone" method that had been so successful at Pharmacia. He received the funding, but he found that there was no interest in bike racing to accompany it. As makers of a synthetic insulin, Lilly instead earmarked the monies for a corporate cycling club that would participate solely in fund-raising events such as the Tour de Cure, a charity ride benefiting the American Diabetes Association. A departure from racing, sure, but still a victory of sorts for Curin, who was now adept at finding money from within and creating cycling partnerships that benefited his company.

After eight years with Lilly, Curin moved to Chicago to work for yet another company. Until he applied for the job, he had never heard of Astellas Pharma. It was a relatively new company, the result of a 2005 merger between two large Japanese pharmaceuticals, Fujisawa and Yamanouchi. Boasting more than $14 billion in assets, Tokyo-based Astellas was in the process of developing its own oncology division and was looking to reach oncologists with its new brand. If that didn't ring bells in Curin's head, nothing would. Cancer and cycling had been sewn together by Lance Armstrong in the early 2000s. Curin's pitch for funds had the perfect set-up.

CONSIDERING THE NET WORTH of a corporate giant it's easy to assume that, say, Coca-Cola or Ford Motor Company could hand over a large pile of money—certainly enough to fund a cycling team. Surely, there must be extra money in Coca-Cola's $56 billion, Ford's $199 billion, or Astellas's $14 billion that a rounding error could cover. A measly $200,000 would not be missed. This is, for the most part, a fallacy. Large corporations may waste money in creative ways, but they have a team of accountants keeping close tabs on where their money is wasted.

In fact, pitching the concept of a cycling team to the marketing department of Coca-Cola or any other company might be the most difficult sell ever made. In the supermarket of sports, cycling is located so far up the niche sport aisle, it's invisible to the naked eye. It sits atop a high shelf out of reach of children and wedged between other sports like rowing, luge, and short track speed skating. These sports get their 15 minutes of Olympic fame every four years, only to quietly retreat for the next 47 months. However exciting these sports may be, the marketing executives of nonendemic sponsors (and even sponsors within the industry) are highly unlikely to back them. It's the participants in niche sports who foot most of the bill. Anyone who has a child playing on a travel hockey, soccer, or softball team can attest to the high cost of participation.

Today cycling has devout followers in every nook and cranny of the country, and bikes are being sold in greater numbers than ever before. Still, the selling power of American cycling barely rises above a whisper. Cycling events such as Tulsa Tough, one of the most popular races on the US calendar, draw crowds numbering in the hundreds and thousands of online viewers but they remain hardly worthy of corporate notice. Meanwhile, the third round of the 2016 Colonial, a PGA golf tournament, drew a 1.4 rating/4 share on television and 80,000 spectators on the course. If you're Coca-Cola, in which direction will you be looking? In the case of the Colonial, west. It's played in Dallas.

Curin knew the many challenges he faced. If there was going to be an Astellas team, there was no way that he could run it while accomplishing his assigned duties. Not only would it be impossible from a time management standpoint, it would also be a conflict of interest within his company. He would need to find someone else willing to take complete charge of the operation. He called former Pharmacia team member, Andrew Frey. Frey had kept himself busy as a schoolteacher and as a USA Cycling official while Curin was with Lilly. He also had a degree from Miami University in a field related to the job: sports and recreation organization. Like Curin, he loved the sport of bike racing.

They agreed that the timing might be right to start another team. If Curin could find the money, Frey, now working as a full-time stay-at-home dad, would have the time and inclination to do the legwork. Curin conducted his own research before knocking on doors at Astellas. He contacted Amgen, a world leader in oncology medicine, and asked for whatever marketing research he could get his hands on linking Amgen's success with their Tour of California to the increased awareness of their brand among cancer patients, oncologists, and other stakeholders. Luckily for Curin, Amgen was quite gracious about sharing marketing information. He was put in touch with Anschutz Entertainment Group, the owners of the event, who were well aware of the challenges Curin faced. Even though Astellas competed directly with Amgen, the marketing goals of the two companies were vastly different and Amgen was interested in seeing cycling projects like Curin's succeed.

Curin also had an insider's view of how marketing money is spent. He saw the corporate year-end reports, so he knew that the Astellas marketing budget wasn't being fully depleted. If he could convince the right people in the correct order, taking into account the interests of the company, he believed he could create the perfect vehicle for promoting the oncology brand.

Such a simple-sounding endeavor took several months to carry out. It took hundreds of emails and hallway conversations to find the right decision-maker who could get the company to move in the right direction. Being told "no" repeatedly and remaining undaunted is probably Matt Curin's greatest contribution to cycling because it finally paid off. In late 2011, Astellas agreed to fund a cycling team.

One glaring error that Curin made during this process was lowballing the budget. When the "yes" finally happened and he was asked how much it would cost, he blurted out a very low $60,000 because that was the amount he had worked with at Lilly and Pharmacia.

"I should have asked for a million," Curin said later, in perfect hindsight. He joked that, really, he should have asked for $2 million, because $1 million is too round of a number, but $2 million would have sounded as though he'd put careful thought into it.

With a $60,000 budget, he was off and running. Or at the very least, walking. Moving forward nonetheless.

Curin didn't consider this project to be an opportunity to carve out a new job description for himself. He was a pharmacist who loved the field and a cyclist who knew cycling well enough to know that his family would appreciate his pharmacological income more than that of a cycling team manager. Anything that he did with the team would be done on his own time with no compensation. But he loved cycling enough to get the ball rolling and find the right people to make it happen out on the road.

He delivered the good news to Frey, whose first act was to establish the Cycling Development Fund, a nonprofit organization through which he could manage the funds properly. As a stay-at-home dad, his strength was his ability to juggle most team duties during nap time. Team members would eventually learn the napping habits of Frey's growing family and would time their phone calls accordingly.

Frey's own racing career began in Toledo, Ohio, at the age of 15. Because he lived only 90 minutes from Curin at the time, they raced against each other almost every weekend as juniors. They also competed against each other at collegiate races within the Midwest Conference. During (and after) college, he worked for a popular Ohio race promoter on several races each year. That led to an interest in officiating, which Frey did for 10 years. His innate desire to help people guided him to the field of education, where he worked as a teacher and administrator until he met his wife and started a family.

A helpful person will find success when running a cycling team. It requires being part parent, part college professor, part circus performer, and part nursery school teacher. Frey also possessed the rare ability to sleep in any position on any surface, a talent that came in handy when there were only six beds available for thirteen people.

Spending many evenings talking on the phone after their kids were in bed, Frey and Curin set out to spend the small pot of gold that they had acquired from Astellas.

CHAPTER 2

ANATOMY OF
A NICHE SPORT

The budget that Curin and Frey had to work with meant that the Astellas team would spend July in Milwaukee, not Paris. To fully understand where this put them on the food chain requires a basic knowledge of cycling's somewhat confusing hierarchy. Major League Baseball and its farm system provide a basis for comparison. Every season, 30 teams compete to play in the World Series. Casual sports fans are usually familiar with Minor League Baseball's structure of Triple-A, Double-A, and Class A teams connected to a Major League team. For example, the Detroit Tigers lay claim to the Toledo Mud Hens (Triple-A), the Erie SeaWolves (Double-A), and the West Michigan Whitecaps (A).

With few exceptions, each minor league team is independently owned and operated. Though connected to the Colorado Rockies by an affiliation agreement, the Albuquerque Isotopes are owned and operated by Albuquerque Baseball Club, LLC. Closer to a cycling fan's heart, the Salt Lake Bees, the Triple-A affiliate of the Los Angeles Angels, are owned by the Larry H. Miller Group of Companies, the owners and sponsors of the Tour of Utah.

Young prospects hoping to make it to the major leagues will usually spend time honing their skills on one of the farm teams. Depending on their abilities, they may spend many years, or as little as a few weeks, working their way up through the farm system. Their progress will be watched closely by the affiliated Major League team, which will also direct their every movement through the farm system. When they are deemed ready, they will be called up to the Majors.

Realistically, they will probably never make it. By most educated estimates, the star player on a high school varsity team has a 5 percent chance of being drafted into the minor league system, and less than a 0.02 percent chance of actually playing in the big leagues.

Cycling's structure is similarly complicated and just as heartbreaking. Its governing body, the Union Cycliste Internationale (UCI), has three tiers of men's professional teams: WorldTeam, Pro Continental, and plain ol' Continental. (One might think that the UCI could find a better way to differentiate between the second and third tiers, but no.)

The WorldTeam or WorldTour (WT) level represents the big leagues. These teams contain all of the recognizable superstars of the sport. WT teams are automatically included in the Tour de France, Paris–Roubaix, Tour of Flanders, and other high-profile races, showcasing the sport's superstars.

There are 18 men's teams at the WT level, each of which is required to have at least 23 full-time riders, four sports directors, and 10 year-round staff members. The team budgets vary dramatically, between roughly $7 million and $35 million. There are no salary caps here as there are for MLB teams, but there is a minimum wage for individuals in the neighborhood of $38,000 per year, which is coincidentally more than half of Astellas's first-year budget.

Applying for one of the UCI's 18 spots requires more paperwork than a mortgage on a house. It includes all the legal boilerplate information, such as the team's annual budget, the financial plan, the profit-and-loss account forecast, cash flow, biological passport antidoping information, and so on. The team must also make a payment of one-quarter of the team's annual budget (or 975,000 Swiss francs, whichever is higher) to the UCI. Essentially, it's a safeguard that the UCI has put in place to protect riders from a sponsor deciding to pull out without warning.

PRO CONTINENTAL TEAMS (PCTs) make up the second tier of pro cycling somewhat akin to baseball's Triple-A league. The requirements set forth by the UCI are less stringent at the Pro Continental level. Bank guarantees and minimum wages are lower. Staffing requirements are fewer. There are PCT teams that are every bit as major league as their WT counterparts, with high salaries, fancy buses, big-name riders, and the ability to give schwag to fans, while other PCT teams barely make the minimums and must weigh every expenditure.

Whether a team lands at this middle level is determined partly by budget and partly by organizational structure. If a team can't meet the requirements of the WorldTour, it will voluntarily remain at the PCT level. Some teams, however, strive to reach the WT level and have the budget and staff to do so. They may meet all the requirements for WT status but are forced to remain at the PCT tier based on the UCI's selection process. The WorldTour is limited to 18 teams, and there is often contention among the teams battling to be selected. As such, the selection process may become subjective, a polite way of saying that it is political.

It resembles England's Premier League soccer, which uses a system of promotion and relegation to maintain a league consisting of 20 teams of comparable ability. In soccer, a team that suffers an awful season may be relegated to a lower level the following year to make room for a more successful team. The difference between English football and cycling is that the selection of the WorldTour's 18 teams is based on many aspects other than performance.

Where baseball has its affiliate agreement linking minor league teams directly to an MLB team, there is no such relationship between PCT and WT teams. As a result, the biggest difference between cycling and baseball minor leagues is that without an affiliate relationship, PCT teams don't act as an official pipeline for young prospects. A rider's ability to climb from one rung to the next is pinned to the rider's own ability to get top placings in races, market himself, make connections, and prove himself to those who are paying attention.

WorldTour team directors are always on the lookout for up-and-comers. They are in tune with what's happening at other races and on other teams, but it still falls on a rider to sell himself to other teams. This is best done by having a résumé full of top race results.

TEAMS AT THE CONTINENTAL LEVEL are on the lowest rung of the professional ladder and are governed not by the UCI but by the team's national governing body. In the case of American "Conti" teams, that's USA Cycling (USAC), which is based in Colorado Springs. (To save energy, cyclists tend to shorten lengthy words. As a result, continental becomes "conti." The amount of time and printer ink saved each year by shortening words is incredib.)

Conti teams must contain at least eight riders and no more than 16. They must have at least one full-time staff member. The bank guarantee is smaller. That's about the extent of the requirements.

It is also notable that there is no minimum wage at the Conti level. Teams are left to negotiate whatever pay scale they're able with riders who are willing. In most cases, teams make an attempt to pay their riders as much as possible within the limits of their budgets, but that is not mandated by USAC, thus leaving a wide range of annual salaries—from zero to $120,000. That's right: There are professional bike racers who receive no salary for racing their bikes.

In fact, some teams require that a rider bring a sponsor to the team in order to be guaranteed a spot on the team. It can be an in-kind sponsor responsible for supplying parts, equipment, or product, or it can be a cash sponsor. This is informally referred to as a "pay-to-play" team, something that is illegal at the higher levels of the sport due to the minimum wage requirements.

It would be difficult to find anyone in the sport who likes these payment arrangements, even among those parties involved. They would
change them if they could, but lacking the discovery of a winning lot-
tery ticket or rich relative, it will continue to happen at the Conti level.
Riders who sign such a contract do so of their own volition because it
allows them to race as a pro. For some, having their expenses paid is
sufficient reimbursement.

During Astellas's years as a Continental pro team (seasons 3, 4, and 5),
the riders were each paid a salary between $6,000 and $16,000 per year.

It's worth noting that women's pro cycling has a slightly different
structure. There are approximately 40 teams licensed as pro teams
by the UCI and ranked according to race results. There is no PCT
or CT level. Staffing requirements are less stringent. The top 15 are
automatically invited to race in Women's WorldTour (WWT) single-
day events and stage races, and as such, they are considered to be WT
teams. The rest are selected using various criteria. The Amgen Tour
of California women's race, for instance, invites the top 15 teams and
fills the remaining spots by including many of the smaller-budgeted
teams such as the American-based Hagens Berman Supermint Wom-
en's Cycling Team, which seldom travels outside of the US to race. If
only a handful of the top 15 teams accept the invitation, there is more
room for lower ranking teams.

SHADOWING THE CONTINENTAL LEVEL from just inches below is where the Astellas Cycling Team took its first pedal strokes: at the Domestic Elite level
of racing, a term that describes independent amateur teams.

Teams at the Domestic Elite level consist of amateur riders who
have obtained the highest amateur categorization by USAC: Category I
for men, Category I and II for women. Another requirement is that a
certain percentage of an American Domestic Elite team must be US
citizens. Teams can have up to 25 members. They are the only amateurs
permitted to race in the Professional National Championship races.

There are Domestic Elite teams set up like Continental-level teams in that they travel to larger races with similarly sized support staff and with similar equipment. They often have generous sponsors or donors who provide everything from soup to nuts: bikes, clothing, travel, expenses, entry fees, housing. It's not unheard-of for these amateur teams to have operating budgets that are larger than those of Continental teams. They will walk and talk like pro teams. They may even drive around in team vans that are shrink-wrapped with sponsor logos, just as a pro team does. They may pay a salary to their riders. From street level, they will look every bit like a pro team. The one big difference—the one thing they lack—is a small piece of paper in their wallet that reads "professional." And that piece of paper changes the game significantly.

While a Pro Conti team upgrading to WorldTour status depends upon the decisions of the UCI to be included in the group of 18 WT teams, a Continental team can upgrade itself to PCT simply by meeting the requirements. Similarly, a Domestic Elite team can choose to become a pro team simply by filling out the license application, writing many large checks, and fulfilling the necessary requirements.

THE FUNNY THING—the thing that is nothing like Major League Baseball, the thing that sets cycling apart from almost every sport—is that all four levels of competition can race against each other on any given weekend. In baseball, each team competes exclusively against teams within the same level. The Toledo Mud Hens never travel to Minnesota to play the Twins.

In cycling, the four levels do indeed cross borders. All the time.

The UCI assigns a rating to every race on its calendar based on the status and difficulty of the race. That rating determines which teams may participate. For instance, a UCI 1.1 European Tour event indicates a single-day race in which WorldTour teams make up half the field while the rest of the peloton consists of PCT, Conti, and national teams.

(That means that top amateurs racing for, say, the US National Team can race against the major league teams of the WorldTour.)

A UCI 2.2 event, by contrast, indicates a multiday event that includes everyone except WorldTour teams. And only two of the PCT teams can come from outside the country hosting the race. Or consider a UCI Women's 1.2 event in which women's UCI teams, national teams, and regional and club teams, as well as mixed teams and junior riders, can be combined into one peloton.

There are several ratings and many rules and exclusions that accompany each race. It creates a confusing organizational chart, certainly, but most spectators are unaware of this structure and really only want to know, "Is Peter Sagan going to be there?" Most knowledgeable spectators are aware that when they attend a race in Walterboro, South Carolina, Taylor Phinney and Greg Van Avermaet are not likely to show up. But when they visit the Amgen Tour of California, all the big names should be there.

The Tour de France is a WorldTour event that, ironically, doesn't receive a numerical rating. It is simply called a WorldTour event. Participation is mandatory for all 18 WT teams. An additional four PCT teams are included in the race by invitation only.

Knowing the sheer magnitude of the exposure a team can get for its sponsors by racing in the Tour de France, almost every big-budget PCT team hopes to receive a golden ticket. As a result, the selection process for the four invitees is not unlike deciding who gets the last wedding invitation. No matter what, someone's nose is going to be out of joint.

Do the differences between the WT, PCT, and Conti levels have an effect on racing? Not really. The earlier versions of the Amgen Tour of California contained Continental teams such as Bissell, SpiderTech, and Jelly Belly. And though the top ten final placings were dominated by WT teams, the PCT and Conti teams were very active throughout the race and made the WT teams earn their wins. The top two finishers of the 2016 Tour of Utah were both Conti riders: Lachlan Morton of Jelly Belly and Adrien Costa of Axeon Hagens Berman.

What is the difference between riders at one level and the next? If they're often racing in the same events, why bother making a distinction at all? It's complicated. While almost all the mystery has been removed from determining a rider's potential thanks to threshold power testing, the line that separates riders at each of the pro levels is somewhat blurry.

Since the ability to measure one's power output has become so attainable, anyone can hop on a properly equipped bike and, through a complex test that involves riding as hard as possible for longer than is comfortable, determine their power profile. They can then compare their result to that of a WT racer. In very general terms, a rider must produce about 5.3 watts per kilogram of body weight in order to even be considered for a spot on a pro team. That number has been well publicized and has become the measuring stick for aspiring pros. It's much like walking through the garage at the Daytona 500 and seeing the same size engine in each car.

That's the basic measurement for a pro cyclist, and there are hundreds of riders who meet or exceed that requirement. Beyond that, intangibles separate the wheat from the chaff and carry a rider to the next level: the ability to actually ride a bike without frequently crashing, the ability to read a race and understand team concepts and tactics, the ability to put one's own needs aside for the advancement of others, the ability to suffer beyond what the power meter says. Important intangibles, all of them.

Riders who believe that it's all about power numbers and race results will be surprised to learn that an important factor in making the team is simply being a decent human being. Who cares how strong or fast riders are if they're selfish, needy, or just unbearable to be around? All else being equal, the small factors can tip the scale one way or the other. Something as simple as being willing to clean the team van voluntarily may be the breaking point between being invited to stay on the team another season and being cut to make room for a better rider. It almost happened on the Astellas team.

But physical strength and racing prowess remain the benchmarks for entry. All the other stuff that goes into being a bike racer comes with experience. The Domestic Elite and Conti levels are where that stuff is acquired.

CHAPTER 3

THE ROAD TO THE MAJOR LEAGUES

Curin and Frey were in lockstep agreement that the Astellas cycling team project should focus on the development of riders. They remembered the struggles they endured as young riders learning the sport, and they both had an appreciation for the mentors who had helped them learn the sport's complexities. This, combined with their commitment to their families and careers, forced them to remain realistic about their ambitions.

Developing strong and promising amateur riders into full-fledged, ready-for-prime-time bike racers is a complicated undertaking. There are many variables at play and a steep learning curve to fit into the fleeting window of a young person's career.

A rider can take several paths to develop into a pro racer.

There's a well-established USA Cycling program to identify talented riders and mold them into Olympians and top-tier riders in every cycling discipline (track, road, mountain, BMX). Regional talent identification camps are held for qualified cyclists under the age of 19 to provide a concentrated period of riding, teaching, and testing under the watchful eye of USAC-certified coaches. Riders who test well and show an aptitude for learning the intricacies of the sport will have many opportunities to advance through the ranks and ultimately be invited to join the US National Team. Contrary to popular belief, USA Cycling's program is not particularly well-funded. In fact, in its early stages, riders must pay their own way.

When riders progress up the ladder, they are shepherded to Europe. USAC maintains a house in Holland where National Team riders live and race, again under the watchful eye of USAC personnel. Funded by donations to the USA Cycling Foundation, the house serves as a base of operations for an intense regimen that leaves little time for outside activities. Riders in the National Team program race their bikes. A lot. In Europe, there are high-quality races taking place three or four times per week and usually within a few hours' drive from home base. In the United States, comparable races are often weeks apart and could entail four days of driving.

The USAC program is designed for dedicated riders who aspire to make it into the top echelon of cycling: the WorldTour. Taylor Phinney, Neilson Powless, Tejay van Garderen, Alexey Vermeulen, and Larry Warbasse are among the riders who have gone through the program. Making it to the WT through other avenues is rare but possible; Sepp Kuss, Andrew Talansky, and Evan Huffman skipped the USAC route altogether and have become a source of inspiration to riders who are not accepted into the USAC system.

Of course, acceptance into USAC's program is no guarantee of success. Riders wash out of the program at all steps along the way for a variety of reasons: school, family, lack of ability, or they simply discover that they just don't want to be a bike racer. Plenty of vaunted riders are tagged to be the next Greg LeMond, only to pack their bags and head home. The system itself is not as harsh as the reality of the sport. It's a grueling existence both on and off the bike.

Failure to graduate from USAC's program is not the end of the line for an aspiring pro cyclist, nor is failure to make it to the WorldTour. Europe is the epicenter of the racing world, and anyone wanting to make it as a pro cyclist will want to experience it. But there is great racing to be found in the United States. Teams like Astellas Pro Cycling exist for talented riders who need another path to the pro ranks.

Believing that race experience makes for the best education, Frey intended to get their team to as many quality races as possible. For younger riders, the ability to travel to a race with a full slate of teammates and race as a team against a high-caliber field makes all the difference.

THE NEXT QUESTION to address was one that development teams must constantly reevaluate: develop riders or win races? These two initiatives are in constant conflict at the Continental level. It's difficult to do both.

Cycling teams and cyclists are judged by their results, just as in every other sport. The podium establishes a pecking order, which in turn affects the longevity of the team. The logical solution is to assemble a team that will win races by hiring a few really strong riders who are proven winners and fill the remaining roster spots with riders to help them.

One problem with the "chasing wins" tactic is that proven winners demand more in compensation. On pro teams, that means salary. On amateur teams, it can mean either a salary or simply getting more stuff (equipment, attention, a bigger share of the prize money, or a private room at the hotel). In other words, it's going to cost something, and in the case of Astellas, setting up the team to win would further strain a thin budget.

Chasing wins also means that the cyclists who ride in support of their team leaders, constantly sacrificing their own chances, won't have anything of value on their résumés. It's possible that their names won't show up in the final race results because they spent everything they had elsewhere in the race to get the leader to the finish. In some cases, a rider's efforts in a given race might even go unnoticed by the team.

For instance, if Racer X gives up one of his wheels to the leader so that the leader can continue without delay after suffering a flat tire, Racer X may be thanked after the race, but a more likely scenario is that the entire exchange is forgotten a few weeks later and Racer X goes one more week without a result on his resume.

A more nuanced example is when a rider slows down slightly in order to open up the gap that soon forms a breakaway. During a fast period of a race, Racer X sees a small group containing two of his teammates form ahead of him and begin to roll off the front of the pack, so he makes a slight hesitation at a critical moment that causes everyone behind him to hesitate. If the riders behind him fail to take the initiative to close the gap, that small gap might quickly grow into an insurmountable lead. If Racer X does this on purpose to create that opportunity for his teammates, he does so at his own expense, and the team will benefit from this nearly invisible action. It's a heads-up move on his part and a subtle but effective move that nobody saw. And once again Racer X is one week older without a top result on his resume.

By the end of the season, a selfless rider like Racer X will have almost nothing to show for having performed little acts like these all year. Team leaders will appreciate this loyalty and will share the prize money with him, but when it comes time for him to look for a new team to ride for, he may not have anything tangible to prove what he's capable of.

It's an interesting conundrum: having just one good result on a résumé can translate into an offer from a bigger team, so riders are constantly looking for the opportunity to win. But if a rider were to focus only on his own results at every race, hoping to bolster his resume and improve his standing within the sport, he would likely be accused of riding selfishly and would lose the support of his teammates.

Frey ultimately leaned in the direction of development while still giving consideration to winning. Over the team's lifespan, they traditionally chose a couple of older, experienced riders to come onto the team to mentor the younger riders and to provide insight into races. If winning were to happen, it would be an added bonus.

BY THE TIME RIDERS REACH the Domestic Elite level, they should generally know how to handle their bikes in the peloton, how to train to reach peak performance, and how to run simple race tactics. In reality, most don't. Since the introduction of power-based training programs, coaching has gravitated away from tactics and toward training the body for the effort of cycling. Bike racers coming up through the ranks are arguably stronger and faster than ever, but few coaches provide instruction in bike handling or race tactics.

At the Conti level, the focus is on racing as a team. Neither Curin nor Frey had the time or inclination to set up orange cones in a parking lot and teach the basics to elite racers. They believed that the repetition of racing was the best way to help riders refine their skills and sharpen their edge. Their plan was to send them to a race with an experienced rider, and let them critique their own performances in the team van afterward. At each race, more lessons would become clear.

Some lessons can only be learned by racing at or above the elite level.

At a UCI road race there is an entirely different world of activity trailing the peloton that a rider must navigate. The experience of riding with a full race caravan only happens at larger races. Not until a rider is in a UCI road race with 30 team cars barreling down the road behind the peloton can he learn how to fetch water bottles from the team car or receive mechanical support. This is standard procedure in the pro ranks and a task that every rider at that level must be completely comfortable with. It's not something that can be taught on a training ride.

Retrieving water bottles from the team car and making it back up to the team can drain a rider of energy that may be required just a few miles further down the road. But it's a valuable skill that must be done several times during a lengthy road race. Learning how to take on eight or nine full water bottles and stash them in a jersey while listening to race instructions from the team director and being passed by other support cars, officials, and photographers on motorcycles going 35 mph is just one lesson. Mastery comes with repetition.

Figuring out how to leverage a hand sling (not to be confused with a sticky bottle) to get back to the fast-moving peloton and carry that momentum as far forward as possible is another skill that takes time. One of the most dangerous maneuvers in all of sport, the hand sling is nearly impossible to detect if done correctly. It's something that a rider would never have done while racing at lower levels of the sport. It requires only one explanation, but repeated practice.

The driver of the support car (usually, the team director) holds a water bottle out of the window. The rider grabs onto the front of the bottle in a kind of backhand motion. At that precise moment, the driver briefly accelerates the car while pushing forward on the bottle. (Very briefly, because the support cars are usually only a few feet apart.) The rider uses the push from the driver to launch himself forward as he takes the bottle with him. This maneuver transfers the car's momentum into the rider and allows the rider to more easily jump back up into the draft of the field.

It's critical that the driver let go of the bottle. It's also critical that the driver not hit the car ahead.

The sticky bottle is both illegal and dangerous, but it happens all the time and sometimes for extended periods of time. Riders who find themselves several seconds behind the main field are sometimes offered a water bottle by their team director as he passes them in the team car. The rider accepts the offer, and both parties hold on to the bottle with a death grip as the team director accelerates to a speed much higher than the rider would be able to ride on his own. He pulls the rider for as long as necessary—sometimes for miles, depending on how far behind the pack the rider has dropped. While race officials willingly accept the hand sling as means of assisting the rider back into the bike race, they will penalize the team when the rider's hand becomes fused to the bottle for too long.

What is the difference? Why does one warrant a penalty but not the other? How long must a hand stick to a bottle before an official will penalize a rider? The answers are at the discretion of the commissaires.

Sometimes a rider won't even bother with the ruse of holding onto a bottle but will simply hold onto the car itself and let it tow him back to the fray. At this point, he has thrown all charade to the wind and is willing to accept any fines or penalties in exchange for being back in the main bunch, where he can assist his teammates rather than remain a mile behind riding in his own personal gran fondo. Seeing as how this is not a legal skill, it's not taught at training camps, but learned by necessity in the heat of battle.

Assuming a rider possesses all these skills and can safely and efficiently work his way back up to his teammates while carrying about 16 pounds of water on his back, the next lesson he needs to learn is when to do this.

While riding for Lotto Jumbo at the 2016 Liège–Bastogne–Liège in his first year as a WorldTour pro, Alexey Vermeulen dutifully dropped back to the team car, loaded his jersey with eight water bottles, and worked his way back up through the pack over the course of 10 miles while lugging about 10 pounds of water. He eventually reached his teammates, only to discover that they all had plenty of water. He had never thought to ask them if they needed it.

THE LESSONS LEARNED on a development team aren't limited to bike racing. Since most bike racers are in their late teens during this phase of their career and spending large amounts of time living together away from home, they need to be taught basic life skills related to travel, interpersonal communications, food preparation, laundry, and so on.

Riders may have to find their way to a hotel after being stranded at baggage claim. Interpersonal communication skills make it easier to beg a rival team for a ride because it's a pretty safe bet that they'll be assigned to the same hotel.

Sticking to a dietary plan while crossing nine time zones and traveling on five different modes of transportation is best learned from someone who has done it several times.

Learning how to efficiently pack a bike is also a valuable skill they will use fifty times or so each summer. And when they retrieve their bike on the other end of the trip, they'll want it to be rideable.

Properly signing in before a race isn't something riders will ever need to do until they reach the elite level. Likewise, packing their bags for a full month on the road only comes in handy when they race a full calendar. Shopping for groceries for a team of eight riders is an activity that they do everything in their power to avoid, but there'll come a time when they need to know how it's done (with three shopping carts).

Fans assume that once riders make it to any sort of professional team, they will have a soigneur taking care of their every need. That they will never have to hang out in a laundromat at 2 a.m. waiting for their kits to dry. All of that will be taken care of by unseen workers.

This is not true. Even at the WorldTour level, riders often pack their own bikes, massage their own legs, and make their own meals.

CURIN AND FREY, along with their compatriots on other teams, weren't looking to build a dynasty. Their team was merely a stopping-off point for riders rising through the ranks, and an end point for riders who had reached their full potential. Winning was never part of the plan. For many of the Continental teams, victories and podium appearances were fine, but true success was measured by the accomplishments of their alumni. Frey and Curin would do their best to provide a platform from which to climb higher. They would dedicate their efforts to seeing any of their charges someday wearing the kit of a PCT or WT team.

CHAPTER 4

CYCLING'S SPONSORSHIP CONUNDRUM

For Matt Curin, the idea to form a cycling team came first. Selling the idea to Astellas came second. The pharmaceutical company now employs as many as 17,000 people worldwide. They make a wide array of therapeutic drugs used in urology, immunology, dermatology, and oncology, to name just a few, and conduct extensive research and development in other areas as well.

In the team's first year, the Astellas Oncology Department contributed the lion's share of the team's budget, so the team carried the name Astellas Oncology Cycling Team. The target demographic for Astellas wasn't the patient who needed medications. Cancer-fighting drugs are not as ubiquitous as those for tackling yellow toenails (Lamisil) or erectile dysfunction (Levitra, Viagra, Cialis, etc.), about which an ad campaign might urge a consumer, "Ask your doctor if Astellas is right for you." Instead, the goal was to increase brand awareness among oncologists, specifically, those who might be choosing which oncology-related drugs they would be prescribing in treatments. According to the American Society of Clinical Oncology (ASCO), there were fewer than 20,000 practicing oncologists in the United States in 2012, so Astellas Oncology was hoping to reach a narrow audience with their cycling team.

The team's participation at races was of little consequence. They weren't peddling free samples of oncology drugs at criteriums or giving away coupons at time trials. Instead, Curin set the stage for Astellas to use the team to interface with doctors through appearances at pharmaceutical trade shows and casual rides targeting oncologists who rode bikes. The number of cyclist-oncologists was admittedly small, but it seemed to be growing. News outlets such as CNN, the BBC, *The Economist*, and *Business Insider* were depicting cycling as the new golf, with tales of business being conducted on a group ride instead of at the tee box. Curin was at the front of this movement when he pitched the sponsorship deal from within Astellas in 2011. And timing might have factored into his success.

The marriage between a pharmaceutical brand and bike racing was a stretch, and the brand was all but unknown in the United States. Team members were asked the question, "What is Astellas?" at almost every single race for all five years of their existence. It's a question that reveals an element of curiosity, though not quite enough for the one asking to Google it for themselves. The odds that the curious fan fell within the target demographic of Astellas were, indeed, very small.

It raises the question of sponsorship's efficacy.

EVERY INCH OF CYCLING is plastered with logos, so the sport has obviously bought into the sponsorship ruse. Modeling itself after NASCAR—if mostly by accident—teams at every level from WT to local clubs have given their identities to outside entities in order to help with the financial burden.

Jerseys are designed to include a main sponsor and any other supplier of parts, money, or services. Cars are shrink-wrapped in a sponsor's logo. Custom water bottles are ordered. In-store appearances are scheduled. Even the socks include branding.

Looking at all this from outside the sport, one might think that a focus group met in a corporate conference room to discuss the proper way to spend advertising dollars and decided that cycling was the best way to get their brand noticed.

It's not. Cycling sponsorship doesn't work that way in America.

Despite all the attention it received in the early 2000s when a Texan was winning the Tour de France, American cycling still remains a niche sport with a comparatively small audience. A relative few who started following the sport during Lance Armstrong's rise stuck around to become cycling fans after his eventual fall. There was a massive uptick in popularity, to be certain, but things soon retreated to a point much lower than the peak. An increase from pre-Lance levels, but a return to the niche sport category nonetheless.

Sponsors agree, and the numbers follow. Although very few examples exist in which a team effectively advertises a product or service, the sport continues to rely on sponsorship as its main fiscal engine.

At the Domestic Elite and Continental levels of the sport, sponsorship is a tricky proposition. The amount of publicity that these teams can amass barely moves the needle. The crowds at most smaller races—local races that aren't given a rating by the UCI—usually consist of the friends and families of the racers themselves. Attendance at a large-scale, well-promoted, national-level criterium may number in the low thousands, but a typical American bike race is more likely to number in the hundreds—sometimes in the handfuls. Smaller races are never televised. At best, they are live-streamed and watched by dedicated followers: friends, family members, and fellow racers who make it to the race.

How many unique impressions—the eyeballs on one advertisement or logo in a 24-hour period—can the Astellas team generate at a bike race on a Thursday night in East Troy, Wisconsin, or a Saturday night in Anniston, Alabama? And can spectators even make out a logo on a jersey that's passing by at 30 mph in the dark?

Once the race is over, only the top three finishers of a race are invited to appear on the winner's podium, while the rest retreat to their cars. The podium is one of the few places where a fan can actually read the jersey. If a rider fails to wear team clothing to the podium presentation or doesn't show up at all, the opportunity to put the sponsors on display is missed altogether.

It seems odd that a rider would work so hard to win, place, or show in a bike race only to miss this celebration. Unfortunately, at amateur events, the awards ceremony is often an afterthought, squeezed in between races or performed during other races. The announcer's call to podium participants goes largely unnoticed because it's a well-known fact (known even by the announcers) that no one actually listens to what the announcer is saying. Many of the racers who are called to the podium are often racing in more than one race per day, so they will either be changing their clothes in a parking lot several blocks away or participating in the race that's currently under way. Or they simply got hungry and left the venue in search of food. Or they forget. It happens all the time. At pro races, more care is taken by the riders to be on hand for the podium presentations, which are usually scheduled immediately after the finish of the race for the benefit of the crowd.

If a team sponsor's logo is to be seen by the general public, it is more likely to happen while team members are hanging out in a coffee shop or while the team van is driving on the expressway. Unique impressions are more likely to be made when a jersey is spinning around in a dryer at a laundromat than when it's circling a criterium course.

Social media provides another avenue for exposure. Team members post photos and updates as well as product endorsements on Facebook, Twitter, Instagram, and other platforms. Tracking the impressions for a post is easier, but it is quickly drowned out by the millions of other advertisements and endorsements. And a Facebook post or a Tweet that is followed by several @sponsor tags and hashtags is largely ignored.

Studies have been conducted to measure recreational bicycling's popularity and growth. Bike sales are tracked closely. The number of users on a rails-to-trails system can be tallied. Participation in races and gran fondos can be charted. But little research has been done to validate a bike-racing team's marketing strength, and the return on investment for a team sponsorship is very difficult to calculate.

How many people ran out and bought a pair of pants simply because a clothing manufacturer named Rock and Republic sponsored a pro cycling team? How many of those sales stemmed from an interaction with the team or by seeing the team race in a criterium? How many of the 300 spectators who were unfamiliar with the brand sought more information on it after seeing the team race in a road race? Weigh that against how much it cost Rock and Republic to send the team to that race. And finally, consider the number of people at that bike race who would actually wear Rock and Republic designer jeans.

Sometimes, however, cycling can be a gamble worth taking. The Mountain Khakis cycling team was funded by a percentage of sales made using online discount codes distributed by the team. Each sale could then be directly attributed to the team. They handed out so many online coupons to fans and riders that the company was forced to change the agreement and the funding mechanism because they were selling too many items online at a discount. It was a rare example of successful sponsorship activation. Too successful, ironically.

The Phonak team raced at the WorldTour level from 2000 to 2006, a sponsorship deal made with the intention of growing Phonak's business in Germany. Phonak, a manufacturer of cochlear implants, was owned by Andy Rihs. By competing in the Tour de France and other high-profile events, Rihs claimed that Phonak's brand awareness grew substantially during the team's existence, though it would be hard to determine what portion of that to attribute directly to cycling.

The team's unraveling came at the 2006 Tour de France, where winner Floyd Landis was disqualified for testing positive for banned substances. The lingering stigma caused many potential sponsors to walk away from the sport. Phonak announced the end of their sponsorship a week after the 2006 Tour ended.

On the other side of the coin, Novo Nordisk, a maker of diabetes medications and devices, joined forces with a team whose members all had Type 1 diabetes in order to demonstrate that they can not only live a normal life but also perform at the highest level of athletics. Novo Nordisk and its sponsorship are as pure as any existing in sport.

Carlson Marketing Group created the Saturn Cycling Team in 1992 after deciding to actively seek out cycling as a sponsorship opportunity for the car manufacturer, a subsidiary of General Motors. The agency studied the sport's ability to reach a certain demographic and the different ways in which it could deliver the brand's message. When Saturn later realized that 60 percent of its customers were women, Carlson added a women's team to the sponsorship program. When they felt they had exhausted the cycling angle in 2003, it was time to move on to other sports such as running and triathlon.

While Novo Nordisk and Saturn are the epitome of effective sponsorship, sponsors who come to cycling purely for advertising or marketing exposure are rare. Most arrive by a variety of different routes, most of which don't involve focus groups or specific marketing goals. Angel sponsors simply write a check with no expectation of exposure or similar return on investment in the traditional sense. Their name may or may not appear on the jersey, and they may derive some benefit from supporting the team, but exposure is not the primary goal.

Investment manager Mark Holowesko has supported cycling financially since the 2002 season through his involvement with the VMG Racing, Slipstream, and Hincapie teams, which stems from his passion for the sport. Hundreds of riders have been given the opportunity to develop their racing skills as a result of Holowesko's loyalty to cycling.

Bob Stapleton, a business owner in the communications industry, was the benefactor behind HTC-Columbia from 2007 to 2011. Michael Drapac personally funded various Australian cycling projects, including the Drapac team, which later merged with Cannondale Pro Cycling.

The Seattle-based Hagens Berman law firm has long been a supporter of national-level men's and women's teams.

A former athlete, Mike Weber simply wanted to help other cyclists reach their potential, so he began sponsoring an amateur team in Wisconsin in 1998 via his company, ISCorp, which provides secure cloud services to a variety of clients. Weber's ISCorp team helped develop former US national champion Matthew Busche and the Schneider sisters, Skylar and Samantha.

For any of these angel sponsors, new business may come about due to their connection with cycling, but the primary motivation is more altruistic. They truly love bike racing and wish to create opportunities for the people who participate in it. Admittedly, angel sponsors are no different from corporate sponsors in that the sponsorship can change course with little warning, leaving teams high and dry.

Another iteration of the angel sponsor is the angel-within-the-organization situation, in which an employee directs money to a favorite sport. The company's decision to be involved in the sport comes not from a marketing committee but from a singular voice. This happens much more frequently than one might think. Many NASCAR, PGA, and tennis sponsorships came about primarily because a key decision-maker was a fan or enthusiast.

Mark Bissell is an avid cyclist and cycling advocate whose family name is synonymous with vacuum cleaners. His long history of cycling sponsorship is a rare but fortunate situation in which the angel within has decision-making authority and understands and makes use of the power of cycling's exposure. Unlike most angel sponsors, Bissell has a popular household product to sell. He has partnered with Advantage Benefits Group (ABG), which is owned by avid cyclist Bob Hughes.

In the case of Astellas, the angel within was Matt Curin, who had played a similar role when he worked for Pharmacia and Lilly. His cause was helped by the fact that he could make a logical and mutually beneficial connection between the company and cycling.

In other cases, a company makes the best of a sponsorship after the fact; the tail wags the dog. The 7-Eleven Cycling Team didn't arise out of 7-Eleven's desire to use cycling as a marketing vehicle. After all, the company sold Slurpees, beef jerky, and cigarettes. Cycling was a peculiar vehicle to reach their target audience, but the 1984 Olympics in Los Angeles were on the horizon and other companies were lining up to build the Olympic venues. Arco stepped up to fund the resurfacing of the running track at the Coliseum. McDonald's took on the swimming and diving venue. By the time 7-Eleven's parent company, Southland Corporation, entered the picture, a velodrome was one of the few venues still in need of funding. As a result, 7-Eleven paid to have one built on the campus of Cal State Dominguez Hills in Carson, California. That partnership was parlayed into the formation of a team with Olympic icon, five-time gold medalist Eric Heiden, as the centerpiece. The team grew to dominate the domestic cycling scene and later became the first American team to compete in the Tour de France.

Whatever the origin, once a company adopts a cycling team for marketing purposes or otherwise, the response within the company can lead to a newfound affinity for the sport.

In the case of the former Budget Forklift team from Australia, sponsorship began as a philanthropic endeavor. At first, the employees were understandably dubious, given that forklifts are not a commodity marketed to the general public as readily as, say, vacuum cleaners. But eventually they too caught the bike-racing bug, taking pride in their team's accomplishments, and the bond became stronger—another case of the tail wagging the dog.

That fact is a testament to cycling's hook. If people only catch a glimpse of it, they may write it off as uninteresting, but given enough time to experience the full excitement of the sport, such as through their employer's involvement, they often become loyal fans.

The reception of cycling was more mixed within Astellas's main office. There were employees who took great pride in the team and followed the team's adventures through social media. Some bought the team kit to wear during their weekend social rides. Meanwhile, an employee in the next cubicle might have no idea that the team existed.

THE QUESTION OF SPONSORSHIP'S EFFICACY applies at every level of the sport, from professional to beginner. Local cycling clubs consisting of amateur riders between the ages of 15 and 60 actively seek sponsors to help defray the cost of what can be considered an expensive hobby. They face the same difficulties in procuring sponsors as their pro team counterparts, though on a much smaller scale. Angels within are the most common sponsors at the amateur level; usually a club member owns a company and siphons off money to the club. The other common sponsorship at this level is from a bike shop or cycling-related company providing discounts on equipment.

Amateur teams will load up their jerseys, shorts, and socks with corporate logos in an attempt to save money and emulate the look of a pro team. It is also common for clubs to use their sponsorship as currency to recruit new riders to their team, even luring strong riders away from other teams. Within the sport, clubs that operate like a pro team get praised, though there is absolutely no correlation between a club's sponsorship status and a member's ability to race their bikes. And in many cases, members of a club that have a jersey full of sponsors often never see a single penny of that sponsorship. It is either absorbed by the club as a whole or doled out to promising young riders.

This phenomenon of amateur club sponsorship is somewhat unique to cycling. In other expensive sports such as sailing, the burden of cost falls squarely on the participants. There are, for instance, no sponsor logos on the sailboats in the Port Huron to Mackinac yacht race.

Where the model for sponsorship of American cycling got its start is difficult to pinpoint. As late as the 1980s, local clubs were very simple: a collection of enthusiasts banding together and wearing very plainly designed wool jerseys with just a few words embroidered or heat-transferred on the front and back. Around the time of the 1984 Olympics, which were the first Games to use corporate sponsorship extensively and conspicuously, and the rise in popularity of Greg LeMond in 1986, corporate logos became commonplace. When fabric sublimation techniques replaced embroidery and heat-transfer, it became easy to create a jersey that looked like the pro teams. No one ever asked "Should we?" They just did. Suddenly, cyclists had an empty billboard to sell to anyone interested, and they adopted the model that cycling had borrowed from the European peloton, which they knew very little about before the arrival of Greg LeMond.

Ultimately, it's up to each sponsor to decide whether it wants to be involved. No cyclist in their right mind would question it because that would be, in essence, biting the hand that feeds them. And barring a viable replacement for funding, the sponsorship model described above is the one that all teams and clubs continue to follow.

Most cyclists are mercenaries—they simply want to race their bikes and have someone else pay for it. Whether the sponsor is a pharmaceutical company, a convenience store, a dentist, or a car company, no rider is going turn down a sponsor that's willing to support a team.

Matt Curin was an enthusiastic cycling fan with the passion and energy to pursue sponsors relentlessly. In addition to working the hallways at the Astellas corporate offices, he also kept his eyes and ears open for sponsors everywhere he went. He knew of the difficulties of selling cycling, and at Pfizer had learned the fickle nature of sponsors. He knew that a promising conversation with a prospective sponsor might lead to another promising conversation that might lead to another, or it might fizzle out immediately. They fizzled out more often than not, but his passion for the sport was a medicinal cure for those cuts and bruises.

Astellas Oncology had what they felt was an appropriate justification for supporting a cycling team. Frey and Curin had what they felt was a pure motivation for doing so. Together, they were ready to make their foray into the sport.

CHAPTER 5

SOME ASSEMBLY REQUIRED

Curin's relocation from Lilly in Indy to Astellas in Chicago placed him in a hotbed of bike racing that dates back to the 1970s, when clubs like Lakeshore Wheelmen, South Chicago Wheelmen, and Turin Bikes were turning out riders like Robbie Ventura, Tom Broznowski, the VandeVelde family, Danny Van Haute, Mark Gorski, and the Meingast brothers: Wolf, Klaus, Herb, and Christoph. In more recent years xXx Racing, Half Acre, Chicago Cuttin Crew, South Chicago Wheelmen, and Athletes By Design Cycling Club (ABD) have continued to drive the Chicagoland cycling scene forward. Access to the local talent and culture would undoubtedly make life easier for Curin and Frey.

On a crisp October morning, Curin showed up for an early morning group ride in the Chicago suburb of Deerfield. The Gruppo Tu Earlio ride is a long-standing weekday ride popular among older riders that heads out at 5:20 a.m. sharp. Curin, at 37, was one of the youngest to show up. Though not entirely out of shape, he figured this was a ride he could join and not get dropped, and he knew many of the riders. Rolling up alongside stalwart Stu Grinell, Curin did his best to casually explain the situation in between gasping breaths and asked how to begin the process of filling out a team roster. Grinell knew that ABD was looking for a sponsor, so he suggested that Curin make a stop at the Prairie Path Cycles on Chicago's west side where ABD was based.

Mike Farrell cofounded ABD in 1992 on the heels of managing two Schwinn-sponsored racing teams. Schwinn–Icy Hot and later, Wheaties-Schwinn, was a cycling powerhouse under Farrell. When Schwinn filed for bankruptcy and its sponsorship ended, he formed the ABD club in the traditional model. It was a large group of amateur riders getting together to train and race, promoting a handful of cycling events each year to raise money to fund an elite racing team. Farrell had a knack for developing riders into top-flight racers. A USAC-certified coach himself, he focused the team on riders under the age of 25 (U25) and produced a number of pro racers through the years.

In 2010, ABD's sponsor, Verizon, decided not to renew its sponsorship agreement, which led to a weakening of the elite program. Riders were leaving ABD in search of teams with more resources. The roster dwindled further by season's end.

The Astellas team needed a base of operations and riders. Farrell had both. When Curin walked into the Prairie Path bike shop with a cash sponsor and a proposal to start an elite race program, Farrell and his co-owners, Mike Ebert and Mary Lee Geraghty, were receptive. Rocked by the loss of Verizon and the subsequent exodus of riders, Farrell was considering doing away with the elite team concept entirely.

It's quite common in amateur cycling for a club consisting of riders at all levels of ability to field a team of elite racers, usually made up of Category I and II racers. It's the first step on the path to pro cycling and an incentive for younger riders to work toward upgrading their racing licenses. With a sponsor to underwrite expenses, the elite team can create its own identity within the club while representing the club at high-profile events. That was the vision that Curin pitched to Farrell and ABD. He would create a team made up of riders from across the country to travel far and wide to race at national events as well as some local races.

Prairie Path agreed to let Andrew Frey run the elite program. The shop would continue to be the bike shop sponsor for the ABD club and the new elite team, known officially as "Astellas Oncology presented by ABD." As the team's base of operations, Prairie Path would provide the riders with a place to meet, handle repairs, and buy equipment and also agreed to provide Trek bicycles. Frey and Curin had hoped to avoid the expense altogether, but the team was required to place a deposit on the bikes and return them at the end of the season. Bikes are one of the largest expenses for a team, and when manufacturers don't supply them directly, local shops do what they can within their own strapped budgets.

WorldTour teams receive between 2 and 8 million euros from bike manufacturers to ride a given bike each season. As part of the deal, every member typically gets two race bikes (one for Spring Classics and another for Grand Tours), a training bike, a time trial bike (time trial specialists often get two), and sometimes a mountain bike to ride during the off-season. Stars like Peter Sagan may receive several bikes during the course of a season painted in various schemes, such as a lovely shade of green to match the sprint leader's jersey at the Tour de France.

Women's teams receive an assortment of bikes as well, usually two or three road bikes. Time trial specialists are typically given two time trial bikes. Climbing specialists might get two ultralight bikes with a climber's geometry.

To help maximize pedaling efficiency and power output, every rider goes through a custom bike fit session. Riders spend time in a wind tunnel fine-tuning their position on each bike, but especially the time trial bike. Throughout the season a representative from the bike company ensures that they have everything they need to race. Should a bike break or be damaged in a crash, a new one is sent out, usually overnight for the big-name riders.

Every team has its own policy regarding ownership, but most teams require riders to return all but one bike when the season wraps up. The remaining bikes are made available for purchase by the riders, but few take advantage of the offer.

Most PCT teams are paid between $50,000 and $250,000 to ride a specific bike, with each member supplied with a race bike, training bike, and time trial bike. The team might provide a fitting session, or riders will have their own expert handle the task. Smaller PCT teams receive no payment but get a full complement of bikes at no charge. Riders are typically asked to return any bikes that are in decent shape to be used again the following year or sold to free up cash, but they may be allowed to keep their training bikes at the end of the season, which many of them immediately sell on eBay.

It's rare that a Continental team is paid to endorse a particular bike, but their bikes are usually free. One of Curin's first lessons in team management was that Domestic Elite teams almost never get paid to endorse a bike, and they rarely get free bikes.

The deposit on bikes would eat into the budget, but the Astellas Oncology team was happy to have matching bikes and a bike shop that was willing to provide mechanical support. Having a trained mechanic tending to their bikes was one of the most important benefits of the sponsorship. Prairie Path agreed to provide a discount on anything else they needed.

Another valuable player that ABD brought to the partnership was a clothing manufacturer. Since the 100-member ABD cycling club had purchasing power, their kit vendor, Pactimo, was happy to provide additional clothing to the elite squad at no cost.

ABD insisted on a consistent look for all its riders, elite and otherwise. The jersey would be mostly white with a combination of pink and blue accents, while the shorts used two shades of steel blue. (Most bike racers refer to past seasons by the color and design of the kits. And as luck would have it, the Astellas team's five seasons produced five unique color schemes.) The end result wasn't as visually striking as Frey would have liked, but it would do the job.

Part of the allure of being on an elite team is the splashy design of a unique kit. The Astellas kit was indistinguishable from ABD's look, which meant that the riders would have to do the explaining rather than letting the jersey do the talking for them.

For Frey, it was a small concession, but another lesson learned.

WorldTour teams have clothing sponsors who pay a fee similar to what bike manufacturers pay, and they give each rider a small truckload of products. Since the riders will face all kinds of weather and riding situations, they receive a ton of product. Short-sleeved, long-sleeved, lightweight, thermal, and every other permutation of their uniform will be shipped to the WorldTour rider, who will unpack the box with the fervor of a child on Christmas morning. This joyous moment then turns to exasperation, because schlepping an entire product line from race to race is less appealing. By the end of the season, 60 percent of the gear has been worn and the rest has been sold or given away.

Pro Continental teams receive gear commensurate with their status. Not everything in the catalog, but enough to provide leftovers at the end of the season.

The Domestic Elite–level Astellas Oncology presented by ABD received a handful of short-sleeved and long-sleeved jerseys, two pairs of shorts, a jacket, and knee warmers. Just enough to look the part. When paired with their matching bikes, the clothes convinced many people that they held pro licenses. They surely fooled a lot of people in the first months of 2012.

WITH THE BIKES and the uniforms in place, the next item on the agenda was to find riders. Fortunately, in addition to the bikes, clothing, mechanic, and in-store discounts, ABD contributed a couple of riders.

Bryan McVey was an experienced local racer from Naperville, Illinois, who had been with ABD for several years and had great loyalty to the Prairie Path shop. Having recently won the Winfield Criterium with a long solo move, he was an obvious choice.

Hogan Sills was a Category II rider with a great sprint. He was racing with the Purdue Boilermakers collegiately and had been a member of ABD for the past two seasons. It was during a spontaneous trip to a race in Cincinnati that he met Frey, who was just beginning to fill out his roster. Also on that ride in Cincinnati was Sills's teammate from Purdue, Joey Iuliano. Frey invited them both to be on the team. Corey St. Clair was another Category II rider that Frey discovered in Cincinnati.

Frey placed an advertisement on TrueSport's website, a casting call for Category I and II riders for a new team designed to develop younger riders. Older riders were welcome to apply to the team with the understanding that they would be in a mentoring role. While he waited for the responses to start pouring in, he reached out to a pro rider rumored to be considering retirement. Jake Rytlewski was well respected on the American circuit, another midwestern rider that Frey knew well.

A hard man, Rytlewski excelled in difficult conditions. During his time on the Kenda presented by GearGrinder Pro Cycling Team, he raced the Amgen Tour of California and other challenging events. Further demonstrating his grit, Rytlewski rode through severe pain resulting from a pinched nerve that went undiagnosed for most of the 2011 season. He had surgery to fix the issue at the end of the season, but it was too late to save his spot on the Kenda roster. Frey invited him to join Astellas, confident that his experience in the professional ranks would benefit his teammates.

Meanwhile, Frey's inbox remained quiet. Only two résumés came his way via TrueSport. Both riders were from North Carolina, with enough race experience to indicate they were on their way up the ladder. Nick Inabinet from Boone and Andre Vandenberg from Mills River came to the team with big aspirations. That was good enough for Frey.

Recruiting riders away from other clubs is not looked upon favorably in the cycling world. There's a strong sense of community, so when an outsider comes in and entices riders away from a team, it's seen as stealing. It still happens frequently, but it can lead to hard feelings that last for many seasons. Frey didn't want that complication, so he never considered the idea, though with bikes, clothing, entry fees, and travel expenses at his disposal, he could have made an enticing offer. Instead, he compiled his roster based on the recommendations of friends in the sport.

Joe Holmes was an Ohio native who had raced with Frey when they were members of the Maumee Valley Wheelmen in Toledo. He had also worked with Frey and Curin on the old Pharmacia team years earlier, filling in as a team manager when they were duty bound at home. Holmes had contracted with many other teams and had maintained good working relationships with each of them. More recently, he had been a full-time manager of the Hagens Berman amateur team, so he understood the challenge of filling a roster and had some knowledge of what talent was currently available.

Dan Harm was one of the riders Holmes brought onto his Hagens Berman team as a guest rider at the 2011 Joe Martin Stage Race in Arkansas. Living in Seattle, Harm was making a transition to road racing after spending three years focusing on velodrome racing in hopes of making the Olympic team. At 27 years old, he was remarkably philosophical about cycling and life in general. Given his experience with track racing, he had great pack riding skills. He also had good nutritional habits that he could share with the younger riders, most of whom survived primarily on fast food. Frey brought Harm onto the team on Holmes's recommendation, sight unseen.

Another Ohio native who would play a recurring role with the team as a freelancer was David Wenger, a former Miami University and Pharmacia teammate of Frey's. Wenger was a USAC-certified coach in Texas working with young riders at talent ID camps and had himself become adept at spotting talent. He had seen plenty of strong riders come along who could turn the pedals hard, and he always wanted to help them fully realize their potential.

Zach Bergh was a 21-year-old from Dripping Springs, Texas, whom Wenger had seen race a few years earlier at junior races in Austin. A disciplined rider mature beyond his years, Bergh had a knack for riding at the racing end of the peloton and sniffing out the decisive moves. Wenger recognized that Bergh needed the experience of racing every weekend, so Astellas seemed like a great fit.

Curin turned to his mentor in Ann Arbor for help in filling the roster. Long-time Michigan cycling supporter Paul Alman had been impressed by a local rider, Adam Kaye, and was eager to find him a spot on a regional team. Curin took the recommendation without hesitation.

Australian Matt Gorter came to the team via a gentle push from Greg Henderson, giving the team some more international color.

THE TEAM WAS TAKING SHAPE. Ideally, the process would have started in July when Frey could go to the races and see who was riding well, but by late November, he had some strong pieces in place: Sills as the sprinter, Harm as the motor, and Rytlewski as the mentor and model of resilience. Buoyed by progress, Frey kept looking for more riders.

Brandon "Monk" Feehery was a hockey player and a cyclist from an early age. The son of an USAC official and bike racer, he had been dragged to bike races every summer. Eventually he started racing.

In 2011, Monk was a sophomore at Lindenwood University in St. Louis, where he split his time between the Gateway Harley-Davidson elite team and the Lindenwood collegiate team. On a random Friday night he stayed home from a party to watch TV. That's when Frey called to follow up on a tip-off from Mike Ebert at Prairie Path.

Monk's nickname had nothing to do with his habit of staying home on Friday nights. As a child he climbed every inanimate object he could find. "Monkey" was shortened to "Monk," and it has stuck with him ever since.

The idea of getting in on the ground floor of a new venture appealed to Monk. He had enjoyed racing with the Gateway team, but also liked the idea of being based in his hometown of Chicago and growing with a team that was just starting out. He accepted the invitation that night. He would be the only rider to remain on the team for the full five-year run.

At the Domestic Elite level of racing, few sponsors care about winning bike races. And since Astellas corporate wasn't concerned, Frey was free to orient the team toward creating a learning environment for young riders. Wins would come, but they weren't the endgame. The team was completely amenable to this approach. At this level of racing, riders are more concerned with getting the chance to race without the encumbrance of having to work a full-time job. With their racing season paid for, they could focus their energy on training rather than waiting tables or working in a bike shop. Riders who came to the team didn't worry about the pecking order or what their specific role would be; they were just happy to have been accepted onto a new team with a comparatively large budget. Had the goal been to win bike races, Frey might have had a more challenging time filling the roster.

His primary goal for the 2012 season was to build up the team's self-esteem with a full schedule consisting of local races and as many USAC National Race Calendar (NRC) races as the budget would allow.

NRC races are high-profile American events open to Continental pro and Domestic Elite teams that attract the best from across the country. The racing is aggressive, notoriously fast and furious, providing invaluable experience to a development team. NRC race wins are highly coveted, so each is approached as a mini-national championship.

A team manager will view a win at a local race with casual interest. But winning an NRC race will earn a rider instant respect that factors into his marketability to teams further up the food chain. Winning the overall NRC series title elevates the rider and his team to a status just below sainthood.

Frey knew that for a first-year team at an NRC race, the only realistic expectation is survival. The big teams push the little teams out of the way. The little teams fight for a place in the top 20, which is a huge accomplishment for an amateur team.

Because NRC-designated races are held all across the country, Frey had to pick and choose which ones to put on the Astellas schedule. Weighing his knowledge of the different courses and history of each race with the limits of his budget, Frey was careful not to burn out his young team with too much driving or too much butt kicking.

CHAPTER 6

SEASON 1: PINK, BLUE, AND WHITE

Most cycling teams hold a spring training camp in February or March, usually in a warm part of the country. It's a great way to bring the team together in a casual setting, put in some quality miles, and get everyone on the same page before sending them off to the races. Teams also take this opportunity to discuss sponsors, distribute clothing, and introduce new riders. It would have been helpful for a brand-new team like Astellas Oncology to hold a team camp, but Frey decided to skip it entirely. Money was already becoming a concern, and camp felt like a luxury.

Instead, he rented an apartment in the Chicago suburb of Lake Zurich for out-of-town teammates. It cut down on travel expenses for the riders from Texas, North Carolina, and Washington and allowed the guys to train together in between races during the season. Perhaps it would be a substitute for the bonding experience of spring training camp.

So the Astellas riders were training on their own for the spring months. Were it a true development team, coaches would have kept close tabs on the progress of each rider, reviewing his power data regularly, but the riders had their own personal "coaches" to help with their power training. And Jake Rytlewski offered advice freely, but the expectation was that each rider would do what it took to prepare. Frey was less concerned about their individual training; it was racing experience that would lead to their development as riders.

Because Illinois winters tend to linger, the riders would have to venture farther to put in their miles. Some of them traveled to Texas, where they could find early-season races like the Driveway Series in Austin. Others went to Georgia and Alabama. The first time that members of the team traveled together was the Tour of the Battenkill in upstate New York. The 13-hour van ride from Chicago to Saratoga Springs was a good opportunity to get better acquainted. Having seen each other at races during the past few years, they were at least familiar with the various teams each rider had belonged to. They shared war stories and discovered plenty of races where their paths had crossed.

The Battenkill weekend consisted of two races: an amateur race on Saturday and the UCI-rated pro-am on Sunday. Saturday's course was hilly, but not nearly as challenging as Sunday's 120-mile test.

The team arrived on Thursday, rode portions of the course on Friday, and hung out in the hotel, staying off their feet as serious cyclists do whenever possible. Curin had opted to take on the role of team manager during their first important road trip. It would be a rare opportunity for him to work with the team that he had created.

The riders were unfamiliar with each other's abilities. The younger riders were anxious to show what they were capable of doing and prove that they belonged on the team. Jake and Dan were anxious to establish themselves as team leaders. It took only a couple of trips over and down a few upstate New York hills for the power meter to sort things out.

They rolled up to the starting line on Saturday, and the unknown sponsor on their jersey immediately drew attention from the other riders. Astellas Oncology looked like a national sponsor and that carried a certain cachet, deserved or not, and added pressure. It would follow them all year long. Particularly for the younger riders, the weight of a national sponsor on their jersey helped raise their game.

The team's plan was to stay out of trouble and use Saturday's race as a tune-up for the next day's marathon. Going with the flow and rolling along in the middle of the pack is no small feat for a competitive person. That plan held for about 30 miles before Jake got antsy and followed an attack by another rider.

The two worked together to chase a lone rider who had soloed away earlier. They never caught the leader, but they stayed away to finish in second and third. Rytlewski was happy and the team was ecstatic to have a podium finish in their first official race. The folks at Astellas might not understand what a moral victory it was, but the team felt validated. They shared the prize money and the bottle of maple syrup that Jake received for finishing in third place, but the next day loomed large so the celebrating was cut short.

Billed as "America's Toughest Race," the Tour of the Battenkill was one of the first road races to include large sections on rough dirt roads. Similar in design to cycling's European monuments Tour of Flanders and Paris–Roubaix, it consistently drew more than 3,000 amateur riders and 100 pros eager to test their mettle on the challenging course, even if it means not finishing the race. The intimidation factor of Battenkill is alluring to riders—the name alone suggested imminent death.

It might have been the worst place to launch a new team.

For Rytlewski, who had been left off the Kenda team for 2012, it was also the first shot at redemption. The race was the second in the NRC series and was rated by UCI as a 1.2 road race, so Kenda was there along with all the other big teams.

Pre-riding the course told the team what they already knew: it was a monster, consisting of two 100-kilometer loops offering eight dirt sections per lap. The dirt sections were dusty washboard roads with loose gravel that wreaks havoc on tires and rims. The sharp, punchy climbs—including an 18 percent grade on dirt—were sure to splinter the pack.

If the riders had looked up even for a millisecond, they could have taken in the genteel side of Battenkill. The course showcased the charm that the area was known for, with its rolling farmland and an iconic covered bridge over the Battenkill River. The beautiful countryside was completely lost on the team.

From the gun, the race went at a torrid pace. Unprepared riders were shed in the first mile. As the peloton neared the first dirt section, the pace went ballistic. More riders went off the back. This peloton included Pro Continental, Continental, and Category I amateur racers. The latter were at the top of their game in local races but were dropped from a race of this caliber.

The Astellas team was hanging tough, which was a good sign. None of its riders fell out of the pack until well into the first loop. Eventually, the pace proved too tough, and Adam Kaye and Nick Inabinet were the first teammates to drop. As they filtered back through the caravan of team cars, Curin made sure they had enough water and food on hand, and plenty of air in their tires to make it back to the finish line on their own. With the backseat full of spare wheels, there wasn't room in the car to offer them a ride.

The peloton was dwindling in size going into the second loop. That's when the rain started. It helped knock down the dust, but the roads became slick and the dust began sticking to everything. Meanwhile, weaker riders went out the back, and the strong riders were attacking on the front end. Eventually, 15 riders went up the road in a breakaway, and Harm and Rytlewski were the only Astellas riders left in the peloton. Andre Vandenberg and Zach Bergh were in the third group and losing ground. Harm hit one of the dirt sections and soon found himself struggling in a whirlpool of dust, cars, and dropped riders.

Life in the race caravan is chaotic in good conditions. On washboard dirt roads in light rain, it becomes insane. Team cars drive three abreast at times. Dropped riders go backward, and riders returning from mechanical repairs go forward. Many of the team managers of amateur teams have limited race caravan experience. The UCI and USAC have implemented classroom sessions with video clips and a

Powerpoint presentation to teach protocols and safeguards, but there is no road test prior to the race so it's learned on the fly. Imagine aggressive bumper-to-bumper traffic moving at 35 mph on a two-lane road with bicycles and motorcycles going every which way. Cars stop without warning. There is a cacophony of horns and screeching tires. Drivers have to listen to the race radio with one ear and everything else with the other. One eye looks ahead while the other watches the mirrors. Riders have the right-of-way at all times whether they're dropping back or advancing. Drivers must keep track of where they can and cannot position their cars. Pro team directors can smell weakness among amateur drivers and exploit it in an instant to put themselves in a better position. Driving in the race caravan is unquestionably the most dangerous but exhilarating driving anyone can perform legally.

Though it doesn't seem possible, the speed of the trailing caravan is always faster than the speed of the race. This is because while the race travels at a consistent 27 mph average, the caravan must slow, pause, and even come to a full stop depending on what is happening, and then speed up to catch the peloton. As soon as they catch the peloton, someone slams on the brakes to tend to a rider, and the accordion gets stretched out again. Repeat ad nauseam. It is not for the carsick prone.

Jake flatted and received a wheel from the neutral support car, which was following immediately behind the peloton. He received a quick wheel change and worked his way back up through the caravan to the peloton, only to get another flat tire a few miles later. This time, the neutral support car was busy with another rider, so Jake stood roadside holding his wheel in the air until Curin found him in the melee, replaced his wheel, and motorpaced him back to the field at 32 mph on a bumpy gravel road. Every now and then, a deep pothole would rock the car, and Jake would swerve to avoid being swallowed up.

While speeding along with Jake in his draft, Curin heard someone yelling and rolled down the window to hear better. It was Jake. The guy riding a bike in the rain on a dirt road just inches from the rear bumper of the team car going 32 mph wanted him to go faster.

Curin slowly accelerated to 37 mph and held it there until he reached the back of the caravan, where he resumed race speed. At that point, Jake jumped out from behind the car, sprinted ahead, and played leap frog with the team cars until he reconnected with the peloton. Avis never intended for their rental cars to be used this way.

This is standard operating procedure in a race caravan. Riders who get dropped are allowed to be motorpaced back to the peloton under certain circumstances. The officials keep a watchful eye on things taking place within the "Bumper to Bumper Club," ensuring that rules aren't completely ignored.

Prior to Battenkill, Curin had never actually driven in a race caravan, so this was his first taste of the organized chaos and heart-pumping danger. With its rough gravel sections and twisty, hilly terrain, Battenkill was hardly the ideal place to jump in, but Curin did quite well. In other words, no one was dented and no cars were hurt.

By now, the peloton was down to about 40 riders. Of the 160 starters, only 59 would make it to the finish. The eventual winner was a former WorldTour rider who had been implicated in, and indeed kicked out of the Tour de France because of Operación Puerto, the notorious 2006 Spanish investigation into doping that involved several pro cyclists. Though the rider had never been served a suspension, whenever a former "alleged" doper wins a race, there is consternation among the peloton. Even the insistence that they must use the word "alleged" sits like a burr under the chamois. Riders at every level desperately want the sport to be clean, and even the specter of cheating is an affront to the riders who race clean. The topic was discussed among the Astellas team members at length at Battenkill and every other time that cheating reared its ugly head during the summer. The collective thought is that if the rider in question needed performance-enhancing drugs to win in the past, then how is it possible for him to win now without them? Is he that good? Is he really clean now? Or is he just more clever at gaming the system? There's no way of knowing. It's wrong but natural to make assumptions. Ultimately, riders must have faith in the anti-doping controls and rely heavily on karma when those controls fail.

The team's post-race discussion wasn't all about doping; it covered several lessons about bike racing, though the talk had less to do with tactics and more to do with survival. Riders determined that their failures were related to poor positioning, which drained their energy for the harder portions of the course. The chasm between Pro Continental teams and Category I riders was clear. Jake had plenty of time to dispense his thoughts on the topic as the team rehashed the race on the long drive home. They were remarkably upbeat. The team consensus was that Battenkill was an unbelievable experience on an awesome course, what little they saw of it.

Had Rytlewski redeemed himself? He had fought his way back from two flat tires and had very little team support in the later stages of the race. This would be a recurring theme throughout the season: it's hard to teach riders how to employ tactics when they are no longer in the race when it's time to employ them. Still, he was satisfied with his race. Some of his former Kenda teammates found him in the parking lot afterward and acknowledged his good result.

The picture of Jake on Saturday's podium found its way back to the Astellas offices in Chicago. They had never heard of Battenkill, and many of them had never heard of Jake Rytlewski. But the company name looked great on the jersey, even if they didn't fully understand what had gone into making it happen.

A WEEK LATER, THE TEAM was headed to Anniston, Alabama, for the Sunny King Criterium. Anniston is another long haul from Chicago, but the race was on the NRC calendar, and it was still winter in the Midwest.

This is typical of bike racers on a new team, especially in the early part of the season. When the competitive fire is stoked and there's nothing scheduled nearby, they find themselves driving long distances to be part of bigger events. No rider likes to have an idle weekend.

Sunny King was an early sponsor of NASCAR racing. His widow, Patty, now oversees several of Sunny's car dealerships in northeast Alabama. Their entry into cycling was community-minded. The town itself had been making a slow but steady comeback since the closing of Fort McClellan Army Base in 1999, which had cost the area more than 10,000 jobs. The twilight criterium is well-supported by the city, which is eager to revive the downtown area. City officials credit the race with playing a part in the downtown district's recovery.

Being a part of the NRC calendar attracts a strong and competitive field to the Anniston event. Adding to its popularity among riders, Sunny King was also one of the first races in the country to embrace the idea of live-streaming. It would end up being a televised butt kicking for Astellas.

The race was a 60-lap contest on a straightforward four-corner course with a slight uphill finish and strong winds on the backstretch. From the outset, the attacks went off the front in rapid succession, until finally the Kenda and Exergy teams combined to form a two-man breakaway. But other strong teams like Mountain Khakis/SmartStop, Jamis–Sutter Home, and Bissell Pro Cycling worked together to reel it in. Speeds pushing 30 mph combined with ripping wind on the backside of the course to whittle the field down. Most of the Astellas riders were unable to maintain contact with the peloton. Nick Inabinet and Dan Harm would be the team's only finishers, in 28th and 34th place.

The ride home again facilitated plenty of post-race analysis. Like the Battenkill race, Sunny King emphasized the importance of proper positioning and energy conservation. On a criterium course with 240 left-hand turns, any effort a rider saves by not accelerating out of each corner pays big dividends later in the race.

Losses make a better teacher than wins. The riders relived every lap, looking for valuable feedback to take into the next race. Even the riders who finished only half of the race distance had been pushed to new limits that they would otherwise never have seen.

Desire and motivation play a larger part in training than most young riders realize. When riders train individually, they are motivated by podium appearances and improving their standing in the sport. They train at a level that pushes their limits, but it generally remains within their tolerance for pain. But racing presents an immediate goal, such as bridging a gap between the peloton and a breakaway because the team needs to be represented, or desperately trying to maintain contact with the peloton. In these moments riders must ignore the power meter on their handlebars and push harder or risk letting their teammates down. Getting into a powerful pack and discovering real speed for the first time is an eye-opening experience for young riders. It raises their threshold and deepens their tanks a little more every time it happens.

ANOTHER POPULAR EVENT on the American road racing calendar is a series named the Memorial Day Weekend Bike Races, held in and around Davenport, Iowa. No one calls it that, of course. The entire weekend is simply called "Quad Cities" for the location or "Snake Alley," a nod to the Snake Alley Criterium in Burlington. The series consists of a road race on Friday, followed by three criteriums on Saturday, Sunday, and Memorial Day. Because Davenport is close to Chicago, it was an easy target for Astellas.

Friday's road race rolled along with plenty of attacks, but none of the riders were able to gain an advantage. A large group entered the final 10 miles without much aggression. Everyone seemed to be waiting for someone else to make the first move. About 8 miles from the finish, Rytlewski pushed a little harder and opened up a gap. When no one responded, he put his head down and slowly extended his lead. Riders in the pack who knew Jake knew that once he had a gap, he would be hard to reel in.

Sure enough. They never saw him again until they reached the parking lot.

It was smart riding by Jake. He saw an unwillingness to commit, and he simply took advantage of it.

Being close to Chicago meant that a lot of other Chicagoland riders were in the race. The win gave the Astellas Oncology team a little more swagger. Not much, but some. It was still only May, and they had ridden well in some important races. Beginning with Jake's win in Burlington, the team was building its reputation in the peloton.

The next day, on the steep, cobbled climb containing five switchbacks that gave Snake Alley its name, two riders from the Ohio-based Panther team finished first and second after breaking away from a powerful field. In 24th place, Monk was Astellas's top finisher.

THE ASTELLAS ONCOLOGY TEAM found themselves rubbing knuckles with the Panther Cycling Team at all the midwestern races.

They met again in Mt. Pleasant, Michigan, at Le Tour de Mont Pleasant, a three-day event designed to fill hotels and restaurants while the college kids from Central Michigan University were out of town for the summer.

A time trial on Friday, criterium on Saturday, and road race on Sunday in 90-degree weather made for difficult racing. Without pro teams in attendance, it was a chance for the Domestic Elite teams from the Midwest to beat up on each other.

The eight-corner criterium saw many attacks, mostly from the Panther and Astellas riders. In the end, Panther's Chris Uberti won the criterium ahead of Monk in third and Jake in fourth place.

The next day, on a flat course through the farmland, the racing was aggressive. The strong wind was reminiscent of Belgian racing, forcing riders into echelons over 127 miles. Fifteen riders abandoned the race, but a bigger factor in the outcome was the disqualification of more than 30 riders for what officials deemed "flagrant yellow-line violations."

It all started when a volunteer motorcycle marshal found himself too close to the field and ended up mixed in among the riders. The riders slowed to avoid collision while the front of the field accelerated. As gaps opened between riders, confusion took over. The riders instinctively looked to pass the motorcycle and get back up among the leaders, even if it meant crossing the yellow centerline to do so. However, the yellow line is formidable, a cardinal rule in bike racing.

Races at this level are held on public roads that are open to traffic. Though oncoming drivers are warned to pull to the side when the race passes, they still have the right of way and often exercise it. This means that cars traveling at 55 mph are passing within inches of a bike race traveling 30 mph in the opposite direction. The margin for error is nil. The yellow line rule may seem like an exercise in common sense, but bike racers push the limits with regularity. When a crash or other situation forces riders to divert from the lane or get left behind, they often ignore the rule. The chief commissaire or chief referee has the final say as to whether penalties are handed down.

In Mt. Pleasant, the decision was swift. The riders were notified that they were disqualified 20 kilometers from the finish. Meanwhile, the race forged ahead across the mid-Michigan plains with only 16 riders in the pack.

Rytlewski won the sprint ahead of Bissell ABG's Derek Graham. Monk finished in fourth place. Though the disqualification of half the field cast a pall on the result, it was another great outing for the team.

Minutes later, a slow-rolling peloton of disqualified riders stopped at the finish line in protest of the USAC official's decision. The ensuing discussion was relocated to a nearby office, and when the dust settled, USAC and race officials agreed that the decision was appropriate. The riders had been warned multiple times in advance of the race that the road could not be blocked by the race under any circumstances. The local police, county sheriff's department, and officials of the Saginaw Chippewa Indian Tribe fully supported the race. However, one township attached this simple caveat to its approval of the course, and race officials had no choice but to implement the request. The Tour de Mont Pleasant ran for a total of seven years without any other such incident.

It was a reminder that, even in a bike race, local laws carry more weight than USA Cycling regulations. And the best way to avoid chaotic splits in the field is to ride near the front at all times.

IN JUNE, A HANDFUL OF RIDERS were invited to take part in the Astellas expo booth at the ASCO conference, a four-day oncology conference held at McCormick Place in Chicago. They would ride on rollers at the booth while a video was projected onto the wall behind them. Rollers are like a treadmill for bikes with three rotating drums, meaning they are not easy to master. The ever-present risk of rolling off the side and launching oneself into a television, couch, or piano leads most cyclists to use a stationary trainer when riding indoors.

The Astellas riders were experienced cyclists, but some took their first pedal strokes on rollers in front of expo attendees. Luckily, no one crashed. They pulled it off like the amateur pros they were. Visitors to the booth didn't pick up on the panic in their eyes as the riders tried their best not to catapult themselves into the neighboring booth.

The riders were treated like superstars at the event. No one had ever seen this type of live floor show at the ASCO conference. And the riders answered a lot of questions about bike racing. They also rode in a gran fondo with some Astellas clients who thought the team sponsorship was a great thing. Even as Zach Bergh and Rytlewski briefly pushed the pace to just below torrid, the oncologists were having a blast drafting along Lake Michigan at 30 mph.

Perhaps cycling really was the new golf.

THE SEASON CONTINUED TO ROLL ALONG without much variation: small victories, minor setbacks. Steady progress for both the riders and Frey.

At the National Championships in Georgia, the team finished in the middle of the pack, happy to have the experience of racing at what is, for Domestic Elite teams, the most important race of the year.

With the help of his teammates, Jake finished third at the Tour of Elk Grove in August. The team went on to dominate the ABD-hosted Winfield Criterium in August. Harm and Rytlewski lapped the field with one other rider and then finished it off with a 1-3 finish.

Frey was pleased to see how the team had become more cohesive by the late-season races. He was growing more comfortable managing the logistics of the team and allocating the money. The season involved a lot of driving, but the riders were benefiting from the miles logged and enjoying the simple act of traveling as a team. Even something as banal as fielding questions from fellow travelers at a truck stop in Iowa made them feel special. But it was the repeated attempts to place a teammate on the podium each weekend, and sometimes succeeding, that was unifying the team.

UNTIL LATE IN THE SEASON, Frey relied on rentals and personal vehicles to get the riders to and from races. In August he purchased a new Dodge Caravan. To avoid looking like soccer dads on a road trip, he had the vehicle wrapped in the Astellas Oncology branding with other sponsors' logos added.

Having an automobile bedecked with logos and bike racks took the game to a whole new level. In a world where the appearance of having one's act together is often as important as actually having one's act together, a wrapped car is gold. It's also very useful. Rental cars and personal vehicles must be cleaned out after every trip, which is a chore that no one enjoys. Having a real team vehicle meant that gels, tubes, water bottles, spare wheels, and other useful junk had a permanent place to live—usually scattered under the seats. Of course, trash, half-eaten energy bars, and dirty bottles also had a place to hide, but they weren't visible, so the unpleasant chore of cleaning out the car wasn't as crucial.

As for the team's apartment, it sat empty most of the season. It would have been easier to have the out-of-town racers stay at Curin's home.

Astellas Oncology presented by ABD fit in a lot of racing in its first year. Based on that fact alone, the season was a success. Jake's results set a good tone. Monk showed promise as a pack sprinter with a handful of podium finishes in amateur races. Looking ahead to 2013, the decision to remain a Domestic Elite amateur team had already been made, more because of financial factors than anything else. It simply costs more to become a professional team. Entry fees are higher, licensure is costly, and rider salaries are a huge increase in expense. If their title sponsor was on board for another season, Curin and Frey felt they had a strong foundation for a second year. Prairie Path and ABD, however, expressed dissatisfaction with the arrangement. They felt that they derived little benefit by having the team travel outside the Midwest, so they decided to part ways with the team. A couple of riders had also expressed a desire for change.

Frey went into the off-season with a handful of things to celebrate, and more holes to fill.

CHAPTER 7

PARTNERSHIPS, MERGERS, AND ACQUISITIONS

The cycling world is made up of thousands of laser-focused athletes relentlessly chasing their personal goals. They spend an incredible amount of time and energy training, recovering, traveling, and racing. When they're not on the bike, they're thinking of the next ride. Bike racers spend very little energy, physical or mental, on anything not associated with the bike or their next race, which gives them a reputation for being self-absorbed. But there also exists a selflessness that keeps the sport of cycling humming along.

Race promoters make up half of the equation because they work tirelessly to provide events for bike racers to attend. Very few of them do it for the money. The other half of the equation consists of the club and team directors who form the teams. Needless to say, they are not motivated by fame and fortune. Matt Curin didn't stand to make a penny from any of his teams. He simply pulled on the oar in front of him because he wanted the boat to move. Chris Creed and Andy Clarke have shown the same determination to drive the sport forward, expecting nothing in return.

Chris Creed is a former Category I racer out of St. Louis who embraced the gypsy life of a bike racer with the Spirit of St. Louis Cycling Club in the 1990s. He slept in a lot of rest areas, ate a lot of six-inch subs, and spent more time on his bike than with friends. While he was a junior racer, Creed's team finished second in the junior national team time trial championships, beating out a strong field and finishing behind a star-studded US national powerhouse team that included Lance Armstrong and George Hincapie. Creed stood on his share of podiums before moving on to real life things: marriage, job, family, golf, etc.

Years later, married and a father of six, he was put in charge of his father-in-law's chain of motorcycle dealerships in eastern Missouri. When the 2007 Tour of Missouri rolled into town later that same year, Creed became swept up in the vortex of the Tour, which he parlayed into a sponsorship role for his six Gateway Harley-Davidson dealerships.

When the Tour of Missouri went defunct two years later, Creed channeled his rejuvenated passion into a cycling team. He partnered with a local bike shop, Mesa Cycles. He worked out a deal with Specialized and later Trek, lined up a clothing supplier, and put the call out for riders. Soon, he had a group of young riders wearing Gateway Harley-Davidson kits around the Midwest. What started as a three-year sponsorship plan grew into a permanent fixture both at the dealership and at home.

Creed knew that motorcycle sales would not spike due to Gateway's sponsorship of a bike racing team, so the team's funding didn't come out of the dealership's marketing budget. Creed simply paid for things as the situation allowed. When sales at the Gateway store lagged, he scaled back the store's involvement and took money out of his own pocket. When the store was doing well, he spent as much as his accountant would allow. There was no set budget.

In the process of financing the team this way, he discovered philanthropy to be a powerful marketing tool. Customers were appreciative of his contributions to various sports programs and veterans' initiatives in St. Louis. The team was an extension of Gateway's outreach.

Creed knew from experience that cycling affirms the values that promote work ethic and fortitude. As a team manager, he wanted to pass this along to the younger generation of cyclists. Gateway was limited to riders under the ages of 23, and run according to Creed's mantra: Coach them up or coach them out. Each rider was guaranteed a spot on Creed's team and given a realistic understanding of his abilities. From there, each rider could decide for himself which exit to take.

Getting the kids to races was the main goal. Teaching them how to be grown-ups was another. Young riders like Monk Feehery, who rode with Gateway for a year prior to joining Astellas, became part of Creed's extended family. Riders from out of town lived in the Creed household, helped with chores, ate meals with the family, and played with the kids. It was an arrangement that benefited both sides.

In more recent years, Gateway has traveled extensively and graduated riders into the sport's upper ranks, including the WorldTour. American riders hold the Gateway program in high esteem, and Creed continues to develop young riders into bike racers.

The Ohio-based Panther Cycling Team is more regional in its focus, though equally devoted to developing riders. At all of the midwestern races, the Astellas Oncology team found themselves rubbing knuckles with that smart, aggressive team. Led by Paul Martin, formerly with the Navigators Pro Cycling Team, and Kirk Albers, who rode with Jelly Belly for seven years, the Panther Cycling Team was in the mix at every race they entered, always managed to put a rider in the breakaway, and consistently finished on the podium.

Panther's president and CEO, Andy Clarke, a Category I amateur racer, raced against Martin and Albers in the Cleveland area enough times to realize that they knew more about the sport than anyone he had ever met. Martin was a national road race champion in 1997 and 2007 and had been on the podium at nationals twice in 2002. Kirk Albers had ridden the Tour de Georgia and the Amgen Tour of California, and had been active on the criterium circuit for years. Both riders were as tactically smart as they were physically strong.

Clarke pitched Martin and Albers on starting a development team while continuing to race. As CEO of a worldwide logistics company, Clarke could direct sponsorship dollars to his pet project. Cycling had set him up for success as a professional manager in the business world, and he wanted to give back however he could. He had also made a number of contacts within the bicycle industry that he could call on to help outfit a team.

Albers and Martin agreed, and the trio formulated their strategy for the team: Keep it small, affordable, and manageable; keep it young; race hard; and allow riders the ability to move on freely. In other words, be a stepping stone to greater things, if that was in a rider's future. A small team of eight or nine riders under the age of 25, the Panther Cycling Team would focus on the Midwest cycling scene, which was strong enough to provide them with ample racing.

The Panthers quickly established a reputation for being an aggressive, tactical team. Albers and Martin were professorial with the young riders, instructing them in the intricacies of bike racing. Because both men still had the legs to be competitive, they led by example on the bike in the heat of battle. Every rider was expected to contribute at every race, and with Albers and Martin out there giving their all, the young riders were inspired to do the same. Even if only two or three of the Panther riders showed up at a particular race, the other riders in the race knew they would be a factor in the outcome.

The team operated on a minuscule budget that was less than 25 percent of what Astellas budgeted for their second year. But a team's budget is vastly different from a team's worth. The value of a team with two experienced mentors, a group of young talented riders, and a full complement of equipment sponsors in hand is hard to tally.

Almost every Domestic Elite team is carved from the same wood as Gateway and Panther. Their funding methods may differ, but they are built on the same stepping-stone principle, not for the purpose of winning races. Since Domestic Elite teams race against Pro Continental and Conti teams for much of the season, winning races would be very challenging for them.

APPROACHING THE END of the 2012 season, Frey knew Astellas would remain a Domestic Elite amateur team in 2013. The decision came down to finances as much as anything else. A professional team must be able to fund rider salaries, a large cost center for pro teams.

There were some obvious holes in Astellas's organizational chart. The team needed a bike shop, bikes, and much more, including some new riders to fill the gaps left by departing team members. The only equipment sponsor that Frey had retained was clothing manufacturer Pactimo, an in-kind sponsor with no interest in becoming a cash sponsor.

With the 2013 season looming, Frey began a conversation with Andy Clarke to discuss a possible merger of the two teams. For Astellas, it would shortcut the lengthy talent search and fill the void left when Prairie Path and others had terminated their agreement. Given his mergers and acquisition experience on Wall Street, Clarke could see some value in the plan. A concept began to take shape, and the riders were notified of the possibility.

Momentum continued to build. Frey planned a broader schedule of races for the team, envisioning that they would race the full NRC calendar or as much of it as they could handle. Astellas was paring down its own roster to make room for the Panther riders, including Ryan Aitcheson, a young rider from Canada who showed great promise. He had the intangibles that a team manager searches for, and Albers and Martin had proven themselves instrumental in his development.

Ultimately, the broader race schedule proved to be a deal breaker. Neither Martin, a practicing attorney in Cleveland, nor Albers, a personal trainer in Columbus, wanted to go back to the hard grind of traveling to bike races. They were willing to race and provide mentorship to the team's young riders, but they couldn't do that from mid-Ohio.

Clarke also had concerns about Panther becoming overshadowed by the larger sponsor, Astellas. He liked the return on such a modest investment, but he didn't want to see the Panther brand disappear from the cycling scene.

By October the merger fell through, sending Frey back to square one in assembling his team. Astellas was on board with more money in the coming season, but the funding would come from the corporate marketing budget, not the oncology department. As a result, the team would simply be known as Astellas Cycling. The company executives seemed happy with the return they were seeing on the investment. Any benefit the team brought to the company was considered a positive return, and customer feedback was good, so Frey was given the green light to continue building the 2013 team.

The failed merger wasn't a total wash. Ryan Aitcheson had aspirations of racing at the national level. He felt that Astellas's plan was a better way to get there, so he came over from Panther.

Clean-cut and well-spoken, Aitcheson grew up with dreams of racing in the Tour de France. With some experience under his belt, he had come to believe racing was racing, and more than anything, he wanted to be paid to race his bicycle. If that meant racing in Paris, Illinois, instead of Paris, France, he had no problem with that.

Mild-mannered off the bike, he had a fierce competitive side that came to life when the starter's pistol was fired. He thrived on being at the front of the pack and raced like a thoroughbred. Frey saw great things ahead.

In subsequent years, Frey received phone calls from other teams proposing mergers similar to the one that he had pitched to Andy Clarke. Having been through the discussions with Panther, he realized that his team was better off doing its own thing.

CHAPTER 8

SOPHOMORE YEAR

With more national-level events lined up, Astellas was no longer positioned as a regional team. And the departure of Prairie Path and ABD meant it was time for Frey to secure a new headquarters, mechanic, and equipment sponsors. The luxury of picking and choosing supporting sponsors and product suppliers almost never occurs at the Domestic Elite level, and seldom is there time or energy to go out on a search for the perfect bike shop or the perfect sponsor. Teams take what they can get. Especially when there is just one person to do all of the work.

Monk was a regular at Goodspeed Bike Shop in the south Chicago suburb of Homewood. He introduced Frey to the shop owner, and the two worked out a deal in a matter of days. The shop would help the team get Fuji bikes at a cheap price and provide the team with discounts on accessories as Prairie Path had done. But their greatest contribution was Matt Kelley, a trained mechanic with aspirations of working as a full-time "wrench."

It's often assumed that bike shop mechanics are simply marking time until a better job comes along. While that may have been the case years ago when bikes were simple, now most bike mechanics receive countless hours of training to learn how to fix these complex machines.

Bike mechanics love the work, though "love" may be overselling it where team mechanics are concerned. Long hours spent fixing bikes, unpacking and repacking the van, gluing tires, and dealing with an occasional prima donna can be tedious. Thus the saying: "Being a team mechanic is a great job, it's just not always a good job."

Matt Kelley loved his job. He could fix anything and had the right demeanor for a bike race mechanic: laid-back and willing to work on stuff that he had just fixed seven minutes ago. Because he had traveled extensively while racing on the cyclo-cross circuit, his travel routine was dialed in already. The plan was for him to meet up with the team whenever they could afford to send him to a race. He would be most valuable at stage races, where time trial bikes need to be reassembled and the bikes generally require more attention.

Goodspeed's involvement was more altruistic, focused on giving something back to the sport more than simply being seen at local bike races. It came as a relief for Frey to have a low-maintenance sponsor.

Having a mechanic at select races removed one more distraction for the riders and it looked more professional to have a mechanic toiling away on the bicycles while the racers were lounging in lawn chairs under the team tent. Once the race was under way, Kelley would hang out in the pit area at criteriums and in the team car during road races.

So as not to put the entire strain on Goodspeed, Frey solicited as many other equipment sponsors as he could to fill the team's needs.

Frey knew a guy in St. Louis who was building wheelsets in his garage under the name Rokkit Wheels. Thomas Heidbrier's company was one of a handful of enthusiastic wheel-building startups that materialized in the early 2000s. A garage or basement full of wheel parts and a box of custom-made stickers and a little practice was all it took to become a wheel builder, much to the chagrin of the spouses involved. As a result, the wheels were relatively inexpensive. When Frey called up Heidbrier, he was happy to be the official supplier of wheels to an elite cycling team.

Rudy Project came on board through a friend of a rider who knew a sales rep. They provided one pair of sunglasses and one set of lenses to each rider. The riders were also given a discount on replacement lenses, although they later found a cheaper price on the company's website. Bright green Rudy Project helmets rounded out the offering.

Astellas was no longer required to match the ABD club uniforms, so Frey gave Pactimo's artists full control of the kit design, which would incorporate the Astellas corporate colors and a more prominent Pactimo logo. The result was a bold kit with large panels of pink and gray. Curin, a University of Michigan grad, died a little inside each time he saw his team in scarlet and gray. At least the green helmets broke from the Ohio State color scheme. It made for a distinctive combination of colors, so the riders had no trouble finding each other in the peloton.

Other national brands appearing on the jersey included Hyatt Hotels and United Airlines, creating the illusion of a big-budget operation. In reality, neither one contributed cash to the team. Astellas simply piggybacked the team onto their corporate accounts. The team was able to save money on baggage fees and grab an occasional upgrade on United flights, but the deal stopped short of covering the oversized bag fee. Consequently, the riders were forced to do what all cyclists do: lie about what was in their giant suitcases in an attempt to avoid paying the extra charge. They rarely stayed at Hyatt Hotels, relying more on host families or cheap hotels nearer the race venues.

It was a meager collection of sponsors in total, but the team looked professional and was ready to race. Frey just needed to figure out who would be doing the racing.

THE TASK OF FILLING out the roster in the second year was made difficult by the fact that Frey needed to make cuts so he could make room for new riders. Contrary to the previous season, when he was taking all comers, he now had to play judge and jury when deciding who wasn't making progress. Some riders declared their intention to leave the team, but most of them held on to the dream of making it as a pro cyclist. His first objective was to limit the team to one category, which would make it easier to schedule races. The four Category II riders, Iuliano, Sills, Kaye, and St. Clair, were left off the roster. Iuliano had already committed to grad school, but the other three had not yet upgraded to Category I, so they would have to find new teams for the coming season.

Bryan McVey was doubtful that he could commit to a full season of racing. Juggling a full-time job with a full-time training regimen was no longer financially possible. Like so many bike racers, he reached his stopping point.

After trading a few New Zealand winters for American summers, Matt Gorter moved back home.

Frey needed one more cut. Dan Harm and Jake Rytlewski were approaching thirty, and the team's average age was creeping upward. Frey decided to let Dan go to make room for younger riders.

With the difficult cuts made, Frey set out to bolster some areas of the team, and with a solid first year in the books, he had a little more leverage. In addition to Ryan Aitcheson, Paul Martin steered another candidate in Frey's direction. Toronto-based Irishman Anthony Walsh had spent the better part of 50 miles in a breakaway with Martin at the Tour di Via Italia criterium in Windsor, Ontario, on Labor Day weekend. Better known in the cycling world as Erie Street, Via Italia is a late-summer showdown between the Midwest and all of Ontario. It's a notoriously long, hard race, and Martin had been impressed by Walsh's ability to power the breakaway away from a strong field.

Frey welcomed the advice of friends within the industry. Frankie Andreu recommended Coulton Hartrich. Since retiring from the sport in 2001 and becoming a live race announcer and TV commentator, Andreu had watched Hartrich struggle on various teams and sensed he was on the cusp of breaking out, but Hartrich was also in a race against time because he was pushing thirty. Having just cut Dan Harm, Frey was somewhat reluctant, but Frankie's opinion carried weight, so he offered Hartrich a spot on the roster.

Andy Buntz came to the team after winning the Category II overall series at the Tour of America's Dairyland, a nine-day criterium series in Wisconsin. His email hit Frey's inbox, along with hundreds of others, after the 2012 season wrapped up, reflecting the growing respect for the Astellas team.

Some emails came from retiring pro riders who were looking to step back down a rung, but most were from young riders like Buntz hoping to land on a better team. Frey received similar emails from every corner of the globe throughout the year, proving the sport's popularity abroad and demonstrating that many cyclists yearn to find a better team, even if it's a world away. Frey found himself wishing he had more positions to offer to young riders.

In October, he received an eloquent email from a British rider who had painstakingly researched every registered Domestic Elite team listed on USAC's website. Matt Green was determined to come to America to race his bike. Having lived and raced in Belgium for a few years, he found the racing there less than satisfying because the riders mostly rode in pursuit of their own results. A former teammate, Australian Tommy Nankervis, spent the 2012 season racing in the United States and convinced Green he would enjoy it. Green put a lot of faith in Nankervis's prediction, and he began his campaign to spell out how he could fill specific voids on every Domestic Elite team. In the case of Astellas, he knew they needed a lead-out specialist who could deliver a sprinter to the finish line. Frey agreed.

Green had been on the podium at some well-known amateur races in France and Belgium, and Frey was hopeful that he could bring a European sense of discipline to Astellas.

While finding a job in cycling is equal parts networking and results, Cortlan Brown found Frey and Astellas in a more roundabout way. A friend told him to talk to another person who, three months later, texted back with news that someone else knew of someone who had mentioned a team that was looking for riders. All those dots connected into something that looked like the Big Dipper. Cortlan had already reached out to other teams hoping to land a spot, without reply. When Frey called, they spent an hour talking about Brown's race résumé. Earlier in the year, he had won the Division II Collegiate National Championship while riding for that perennial powerhouse, the Salt Lake Community College team. He and another rider had dropped the entire field on the toughest climb of the day, and Brown took the two-up sprint at the finish. That was good enough for Frey. Brown was signed a few days later.

The final addition was the 2011 Elite National Road Race champion, Max Korus, a former Ivy League runner at Penn. Smart and talented with loads of natural ability, Korus won his national championship in his second year of racing for BikeReg.com-Cannondale on a hot day on a demanding course. While working for another teammate, he covered a late-race breakaway that ended up staying away to the end. This proved to Frey that Korus had the ability to work selflessly and take care of business should the opportunity present itself.

The second season marked a turning point for the team. The addition of Green, Hartrich, and Walsh meant that Astellas now had some guns that could be a factor in many races. In young riders like Brown, Korus, and Aitcheson, Frey could see the future of the team taking shape. He had a core group of young riders dedicated to making it in the sport. It felt like a true development team with riders who were poised to benefit from concentrated race experience.

WITH MORE MONEY in the bank in 2013 (about $125,000), Frey decided to hold a spring training camp in South Carolina. In previous years the national championships were held in Greenville, and Jake Rytlewski knew of several routes in the hills surrounding the city.

Frey was still a one-man band in the home office, running the organization from a laptop in the living room. He was getting better at moving ten riders around the country efficiently and cheaply, but he relied heavily on the flexibility and patience of the riders.

Cortlan Brown stepped off the plane at the Greenville-Spartanburg airport excited by the prospect of racing for a national team. Prior to this, he had only traveled outside Utah with his bicycle on two occasions. Brown hadn't met any of his teammates and he had no idea where he was going, but he trusted that the team van would be waiting at the curb when he walked out of baggage claim.

Two hours later, he was still waiting. It was his first test of cycling travel logistics. If he wanted a career in bike racing, he would have learn how to wait at the curb outside baggage claim.

Meanwhile, Rytlewski and the rest of the campers drove down from Chicago in the team van packed so tight that passing cars might have guessed they were escaping an overthrown government. With six riders, six bikes, ten bike bags, personal gear, coolers, and spare wheels, there only five seats. They took turns sitting on the floor during the 13-hour drive, and arrived at the airport in time to pick up Brown just before he reached the point of panic. He was crammed into the remaining space in the van, and they sped off to find their hotel.

Though the team was sponsored by Hyatt, Astellas Corporate also had a relationship with Marriott hotels, which they shared with the team in a nonsponsor role. Word that they were booked at the Marriott reached the team after they had already unloaded the van and tried to check into the Hyatt in Greenville. Regardless of the change in plans, they were relieved to know that they would have decent accommodations after such a long drive. On arriving at the Marriott, they discovered there was a shortage of rooms and the riders would have to share a king-sized bed with a teammate. There is not a racer in this world who hasn't received the same surprise at check-in.

Greenville is located in the foothills of the Blue Ridge Mountains. Jake set his sights on the two highest points in South Carolina, Paris and Sassafras Mountains. Each day consisted of three- and four-hour rides on terrain that was decidedly more challenging than his teammates were expecting for early-season riding. Eventually they intervened to let Jake know he was drilling them too hard.

After five days on the bike and plenty of time sitting around the hotel, it was clear that there was a good mix of eccentricities on the team, without the egocentricities that cause complications. Credit Andrew Frey for putting together a group of guys capable of developing camaraderie. Their banter was equal parts playful jabs and sophomoric movie references. In an effort to bring the foreign riders in on the fun, they fit in a late-night viewing of *Deliverance* before heading to bed.

Since Matt Kelley didn't make it to training camp, Andy Buntz pitched in to assemble Anthony Walsh's time trial bike. Having spent a fair amount of time completing the project, he proudly handed it off to Walsh, proclaiming it was "good to go!" Walsh hopped on and over the course of his first ride, the seat post slipped, the brake cables pulled free, the handlebars tilted down, and the stem turned freely on the steering tube. Buntz's "good to go" became the team's sardonic rallying cry.

CHAPTER 9

SEASON 2: PINK AND GRAY

At the conclusion of training camp, most of the team headed south to Tampa for the Cigar City Brewing Criterium, a nighttime race and a fixture on USA Cycling's National Criterium Calendar (NCC) that attracted all the big American teams. Fortunately, the van had enough seats for everyone making the trip.

Like many of the younger riders on the team, Cortlan's mind was consumed with anticipation as he warmed up prior to the race. He had been in plenty of bike races before, but this was his first race with so many pro riders. During the off-season, he had pushed himself to significantly increase his training volume because he knew that jumping from a regional team that seldom left Utah to an elite team racing nationally would require more of everything. More speed, more endurance, and better bike-handling skills.

Prior to the race, the team had discussed the expected speeds of the race, but he knew that no words could prepare him for the reality of racing at the elite level. Of this he was sure—he was about to get hammered silly by the United Healthcare and SmartStop–Mountain Khakis teams.

The pro teams drove a blistering fast race and Cortlan stared in disbelief at the new high speeds registering on his computer. Most of all, he was relieved to discover his training prepared him to move effectively around in the pack and hold his position when the pace picked up. At some point in their development, riders reach a point where they begin playing the game of high-speed chess without worrying about running out of gas. Until then, they must measure their efforts and be vigilant about closing the gaps forming right in front of them. With improved speed and endurance, they can break out of survival mode and really race.

In any race, at any level, there are riders in the pack who are doing their best just to hang on and not get dropped. There are others who hope for a lucky break. They know they have just one bullet to fire and they pray it lands them in the winning breakaway. Then there are riders who seem to have plenty of bullets and the ability to fire them off at will.

At no point was Brown in danger of being dropped. In fact, he never saw the back of the pack. He had plenty of bullets, but he wasn't sure when to fire them. What eventually took him out of the race was a crash just past the midway point. Crashes also sidelined Aitcheson, Walsh, and Buntz.

United Healthcare took the win. Astellas was disappointed in its early-season debut, but they managed to be competitive with the pro teams. For Astellas, racing Cigar City was akin to drinking from the fire hose. Intimidating, but not impossible. It was a milestone that brought confidence that would carry them through the season. Had they been dropped or otherwise humiliated, however, it would have taken them a long time to recover.

Finishing in 24th place, Matt Green didn't end up in the money, but he was the top Astellas rider. And he had fun, an unexpected outcome that was worth plenty.

THE TEAM'S PERFORMANCE at the Redlands Classic in California a couple of weeks later was less fruitful. Following wheels all day (letting others dictate the race), the team struggled to finish each stage—but they loved it. Racing in Southern California was an exotic experience for East Coast and northern riders who were accustomed to pine trees, not palms. Redlands is marked in red on most teams' schedules because it is more prestigious than most of the other multiday races on the calendar. For the Astellas team, it would be a week of head-banging in which they could only hope to sit in and learn.

This is where the philosophy of the team insulated them from failure. After all, this team wasn't built to win those races but to provide the riders with experience that would serve them well further up the road. If they learned nothing more than what other riders were capable of or what to expect on a major climb like the one up to Oak Glen, it served a purpose. If a rider learned something about himself during the week, all of them were winning.

Monk, whose expertise was sprinting, was not in contention in the final gallop, but he deduced that to be in contention on the last lap of the downtown criterium, he had to position himself in the top four riders going into the final three turns. Any farther back and he would have no opportunity to pass in the frantic run-up to the finish. He filed that away for later use.

IN MAY, THE TEAM TOOK their first trip abroad to race in the Rás Tour of Ireland. Irishman Anthony Walsh made the trip happen. Before coming to the States he had worked with Cycling Ireland, Ireland's cycling federation, so he used those connections to facilitate the team's visit.

In Ireland, the Astellas team was present at the front of the race each day and was represented in almost every breakaway. Ryan, Jake, and Coulton each made forays off the front of races.

At one point up Cortlan looked around and realized that he was off the front of a bike race in Ireland, and it wasn't a dream. These weren't the usual suspects he raced against back home. These bike racers aspired to compete in the Tour de France someday. And surely, some of them would. It was surreal experiencing the high of achieving a dream in the very moment it was playing out.

The Rás Tour of Ireland held a different fate for Green, who missed a turn on a descent, slid off the road, and went down a small embankment, breaking three ribs. His luck took another hit a few weeks later when he contracted pneumonia, and fluid began to build up in his lungs.

Until Green's crash, the team was enjoying their time in Ireland. The other teams were very welcoming and the racing was exhilarating. Ryan and Jake finished side by side in 34th and 35th place, respectively, but they weren't able to get a stage win. On the international scene, they were amateurs playing the role of the aggressor but weren't quite ready for big-time racing.

While in Ireland, the team was invited to represent Astellas at an ASCO function. They showed up with their bikes and wore their kits and awkwardly made small talk with the attendees. The riders were unsure what was expected of them, and the attendees were equally baffled as to who these quiet, skinny guys were. Then Matt Green picked up the microphone and started talking about bike racing. It was the icebreaker the soiree needed and from that point on, the sales reps were captivated.

Still more needed to be done to capitalize on the strength of cycling, but there was some question as to how to reach latent cycling fans. The evening in Ireland suggested it was possible, but there remained a disconnect between what the team could bring to the company and what the company needed from the team.

CORTLAN BROWN WENT HOME and raced locally in Utah for a month. It was his first opportunity to race against his old friends wearing his new team kit and he quickly discovered how hard it is to return to the old neighborhood. Everyone wanted to test their mettle against the pro. And even though Cortlan wasn't a pro rider, the local riders looked at him as such because he was racing nationally on someone else's dime. The distinction between pro and elite amateur is often lost on amateur riders. They might be unfamiliar with cycling's various levels, or they don't realize that there is a different license for pro riders, or they simply don't care. The fact that a rider is on a "real team" says more than his license.

Without his teammates, Cortlan could never find the podium in any of the races he entered. Every time he tried to join a breakaway, the other riders would sit up when he caught up to them. Every time he attacked, they chased him down. The other teams would wear him down with constant attacks, and slip away when he could no longer respond.

He understood that it was a sign of respect. He had become one of the big dogs, like the guys he looked up to when he was younger. Still, it was frustrating to be marked every time he got out of the saddle.

He rejoined his team in time for an appearance at the ASCO annual meeting in Chicago. The conference consisted of panel discussions with titles like "The Conundrum of Clinically Meaningful Benefit" and "Vitamin D Deficiency in Pancreatic Cancer"—nothing a bunch of cyclists could speak directly to. There was one panel discussion that seemed to invoke cycling terminology: "Physicians Hit the Barricades over Cancer Costs." Alas, it was just as far afield as the others.

The team was invited to appear at the Astellas booth as, for lack of a better term, a conversation starter. They set up a few sets of rollers again as they had the year before, and the riders took turns putting in stationary miles. Curious onlookers paused long enough to become ensnared by Astellas's representatives. But any conversations the attendees had with riders were again stilted. The disconnect was obvious to the riders, but there was no one to help bridge the gap.

When WorldTour teams make public appearances, a media relations specialist usually accompanies them to ensure that the message is presented clearly. Armed with media guides and information packets, they are careful to ensure that cycling and its sponsors are represented properly to anyone who shows interest in the team. This smooths the awkwardness of putting the athletes in front of people with whom they have little in common.

STILL RECOVERING FROM PNEUMONIA, Green hopped in the van with Cortlan and drove 18 hours to Quebec for the Tour de Beauce. They planned to ride for a few days before the rest of the team flew in for the race. On arrival, they found that their only housing option was a single room above a pub in a seedy part of town. The manager was apologetic when he learned that they were staying overnight; the room normally only rented out for a few hours at a time. It had one queen bed.

Beauce, as it's known among racers, is billed as the oldest stage race in North America, which is better than the more accurate description— the hardest race that American cycling fans have never heard of. It stands in the shadow of the other stage races, but it turns out hardened champions, several of whom would go on to race with WorldTour teams: Svein Tuft, Rory Sutherland, Nate Brown, Henk Vogels.

For the younger Astellas riders, Beauce was a reminder that racers race no matter what the weather is doing. At Beauce, it was solid rain. Racing in the rain is a skill much like sprinting or climbing. Some riders hate getting wet or managing the slippery feeling under their wheels, and they mentally check out when the first raindrop hits the ground. Having raced extensively in wet conditions in the UK, Walsh and Green gave their teammates tips on how to get over it.

Amazingly, pneumonia-ridden Green was the top finisher, in 63rd place. Hartrich was the next Astellas rider a few places back.

Day two brought more rain and a 150 km slog. It was the kind of day that could make anyone reconsider career choices. Korus rode well and grabbed 13th place in the field sprint. The next Astellas rider was Cortlan, in 52nd place.

The third stage was the queen stage, or signature stage, finishing with a 6 km climb up Mont Mégantic with an average gradient of 18 percent. It was a climb that left some riders to finish more than 50 minutes behind the winner. For Astellas, Cortlan and Coulton finished side by side in 33rd and 34th place, just 4 minutes behind.

The rest of Beauce followed the same theme of hard racing in bad weather. By the end of stage 5, Green and Aitcheson had bailed. Aitcheson had spent a good portion of the season away from the team, racing with the Canadian U23 National Team at big events such as the Tour of Alberta and the U23 versions of the Tour of Flanders and Liège–Bastogne–Liège. The season was well under way, but he was just getting acquainted with his Astellas team.

On the sixth and final stage, Cortlan was behind a rider who decided to bunny-hop a pothole without warning. Potholes are a rude surprise, but this is one of the most selfish moves a rider can make. A simple shout prior to launch gives the next rider a moment's notice, which can make all the difference. The same thing had happened at the national championships a few weeks earlier. A rider had hopped over a pothole, and Cortlan rear-ended him. The crash ripped the cleat off the bottom of his shoe, but Jake stopped and insisted on lending Cortlan a shoe to continue racing. But this time, the rider didn't stick the landing and crashed in front of Cortlan, causing him to tumble. Jake ran into the back of Cortlan's bike and went down even harder, breaking his collarbone. Rather than go to the hospital, he insisted on simply wrapping his arm and toughing it out. Having broken his collarbone before, he knew how to treat it himself. Part of the treatment was not to tell anyone, including his wife.

Stage 6 claimed everyone but Hartrich, who saw it through to the bitter end. Oddly, having just one finisher was a satisfactory result for the team in a race that sees only a few riders finish.

The team was cracked from five days of hard racing. Korus joined Brown and Green to make the road trip back to Chicago, but the van broke down 20 miles into the trip and had to be put on a flatbed and transported back to town.

The flatbed operator insisted that it was against the law to carry more passengers than the cab had seats. According to him, the fine for getting caught was $15,000 Canadian dollars, which is either $27 or $18,000 American dollars, depending on which rider you ask. Someone would have to hitchhike. The riders were not about to leave a teammate, so they verbally agreed to send Korus hitchhiking to the next town and then created a diversion so he could jump up onto the flatbed and hide in the team van for the duration of the trip. It was a brilliant move, even if the flatbed driver saw it all go down and simply pretended not to notice.

Max got the better end of the deal, given that he could stretch out on the van's bench seats on the way back to Beauce.

AS THE SEASON ROLLED ON, Frey was busy orchestrating the logistics and spending a lot of money on gas and tolls, but the team was racing. A lot.

Matt Green emerged as a team leader by virtue of doing most of the driving, but he was wearing his body down physically. He hadn't stopped since coming to the United States in March. After training camp, he and Jake spent two nights in Tampa and a couple of days in Delray Beach, and then drove the car to Indy, to Boulder, out to Redlands, through the night to Indy via Chicago to pick up equipment, and then down to Arkansas, never staying anywhere for more than a couple of days at a time. Green flew to Ireland for the RAS Tour of Ireland, where he may have cheated death, and then returned to Indy for a hospital visit (the same hospital, incidentally, made famous by Betsy Andreu and Lance Armstrong), where he finally learned just how serious his problems were. After what he refers to as the "night of a thousand nurse visits," he was discharged and went directly to the ASCO conference in Chicago, where he and Rytlewski had to smile at strangers for four days before heading to Beauce, where Jake crashed and broke his collarbone.

Every elite cyclist shares a similar story. It's a badge of honor to be able to rattle off a demanding schedule that includes long drives that crisscross the country, delayed flights, crashes, illness, sketchy hotels, and hard racing. But it usually ends with a solid week of suffering in a bed-ridden hell.

For Matt, the meltdown happened at the Tour of America's Dairyland (TOAD). The effects of 91 straight days on the road finally caught up with him. He didn't last more than seven laps in any of the races he entered.

TOAD is a 10-day event consisting solely of criteriums in small towns within a shout of Milwaukee. It echoes the former Superweek race series, which ran from 1967 to 2012. The driving is minimal, but the racing is demanding. Despite his inability to contribute to his team's performance, this is where Green fell in love with the criterium format. He hadn't raced anything like it in England. He had done a few criteriums in his travels, but TOAD was a concentrated session on fast, friendly venues.

Green discovered that American criterium racers have developed a different skill set from their European counterparts because of the nature of the courses themselves. European roads are generally more narrow and nearly void of 90-degree turns, so every approach is slightly different, which requires riders to take them a little slower. Furthermore, they don't ride multiple laps as in a criterium, so they're basically sight-reading every corner, seeing it just a few times, or never seeing it again. Streets in American towns, in contrast, are wider and almost exclusively squared off at 90-degree angles, making the entry apex far more predictable. Riding multiple laps on the same course, American riders can throw themselves into each turn with reckless abandon, knowing that the exit apex is going to be where they expect it to be. As a result, the criterium specialists in the States have honed their cornering skills to the point at which they race the crit course like a flattened velodrome without ever touching the brakes.

For Green, the American crit was a mind-blowing experience.

Monk, however, was raised on American criteriums. He knew how to race them, not with brazen fearlessness but with calculated movements, knowing when to go to the front and when to hang back. He was also developing a sixth sense for breakaways and gaining confidence in the final sprints. His secret: Don't react to what others are doing; be the one doing the doing. His less crit-savvy teammates marveled at his ability to stick his nose into gaps that didn't seem big enough. Nobody saw how hard he worked at those skills during the off-season.

ASTELLAS WAS NO LONGER a new team struggling to find its place in the world. Their hectic schedule made them seasoned veterans before the 4th of July. Their routines were dialed in. The grind of travel had smoothed the rough edges, and they moved with a confidence that belied the fact that they were still sophomores in the bike racing world. It was exactly what Frey and Curin had hoped to see.

They were bagging experiences more than race wins, but they felt they had procured just enough of both to warrant a conversation about upgrading to the pro ranks for the 2014 season. Curin and Frey discussed it at length before Curin pitched the idea to the check writers at Astellas. When he finally got their blessing, Frey started the paperwork that would make Astellas a professional team. The forms were submitted just hours before the deadline.

As for the riders, the end of the 2013 season couldn't come fast enough. Everyone was exhausted from racing so much, but it was the countless hours in the team van that delivered the knockout punch.

CHAPTER 10

ORCHESTRATING A BIKE RACE

The mechanics of a bike race are like the story of stone soup; each member of the community contributes to the effort. Eventually, where once there was nothing, an elaborate feast appears.

Like a boxing promoter or a concert promoter, a bike race promoter puts together a race and oversees it from beginning to end. The titles "race director" and "promoter" are used interchangeably to refer to the person (or a team of people) willing to take on a thankless role. They are in charge of laying out the course, arranging the road closures, gathering permits, lining up the officials, hiring an announcer, procuring emergency responders, and handling all the tasks that turn an empty stretch of road into a bike race. This includes all the paraphernalia, too—from the bib numbers and safety pins to the placement of the porta-johns in the parking lot, usually just a little too far from the starting line.

Anyone wishing to promote a bike race in their town need only pick up the phone and make a few thousand phone calls. The first 500 calls will be placed to prospective sponsors asking them for money because without funding, it's an impossible dream. Once sponsorship is secured, the next phone call should be to the local government to acquire the necessary permission to use specific roadways.

In the form of an example, suppose a make-believe promoter has decided to bring a criterium to downtown Yourtown, USA, on May 1.

In conversations at City Hall, it is discovered that the mayor of Yourtown is a huge bike-racing fan—he has actually been to the Tour de France, though it was only while he was in Paris for a wedding and he didn't get to actually see the race—he loves the idea and is excited to bring all the biggest names in American cycling to town, but he insists on making one very small change: "Let's hold the race on June 1 to coincide with the Yourtown Pickle Festival."

OK, fine. If that's what it takes to get his approval, so be it.

That minor change is important because it indicates that the date of the race is dictated by a force completely unrelated to cycling: the whim of the mayor and his love of pickles. Or his love of pickle festivals.

The Yourtown City Council gets on board and approves the idea of bringing a special event to town. The public works director has approved the overtime for his crew to work on a Sunday to erect road barricades. Things look good for the Yourtown Cycling Classic (which cyclists will shorten to simply the "Yourtown Crit" or "Yourtown," or even "Yourt"). The race director has even found a sponsor: "Fictitious, Inc.," maker of fine widgets.

Let's pretend (wildly) that our sponsor Fictitious, Inc., has provided a pile of money to put on this cycling event. Thousands of dollars. It's going to be a killer event. The winner will receive a gold-plated Fictitious widget.

The next call that needs to be placed is to the USAC offices in Colorado Springs to secure a race permit. This permit is almost a rubber stamp. After a check to see that there are no conflicting races being held nearby on the same date, USAC will grant a permit that simply indicates that USAC will be the governing body, and that the races will be held in accordance with USAC rules. As such, all racers who attend will be required to hold a USAC license. USAC race officials will be assigned to the event to ensure competitors comply with the rules.

Had there been a conflict with a nearby event, USAC would encourage the race director to consider changing the date, but likely wouldn't withhold the permit. If they did, the promoter would need to convince the mayor to change the date.

The promoter and crew have a lot of freedom in producing the event. USAC's involvement is almost exclusively limited to the rules of the race itself and the participants therein. They will advise the promoter on aspects of the race such as preparing an on-site emergency preparedness plan or notifying hospitals of potential incoming patients in the event of a crash. Depending on the size of the event, they may send a representative to be present on race day.

The promoter must design the course, taking into account many things such as traffic patterns, crowd management, competitiveness, and rider and spectator safety. USAC provides specific guidelines for course design, but it is understood that the promoter has to work within the scope of what Yourtown is willing to offer.

When it comes to advertising the race to attract riders, it's primarily up to the promoter to get the word out about the big bike race in Yourtown on June 1. In addition to the Picklefest website, they'll put it on Facebook and other social media. They may print up flyers and stick them on windshields in the parking lot at other races. They will likely use an online registration resource that will also advertise the race. (USAC provides this service, but the promoter is not obligated to use it.) Otherwise, USAC will only list the basic information on its website: date, time, location, and URL.

The promoter can spend money on the event's production elements, such as a fancy finish-line venue with fencing, signage, tents, grandstands, and other amenities to make the event as grand as possible: food vendors, live entertainment, expo area, petting zoo, dunk tank, VIP area, and so on. But the true selling point of the race—the thing that will help word of the race spread like wildfire throughout the cycling community—will be the prize list: the amounts of money awarded to the top finishers. USAC provides guidelines for payout schedules based on the size of the event and the money budgeted for prizes. Quite simply, a bigger prize list generally attracts more riders.

In the Yourtown Crit example, thanks to the generosity of Fictitious, Inc., the prize list will be large for all fields: Pro Men, Elite Women, Elite Men, Women, Masters, Categories III, IV, and V, and Juniors.

Since this fictitious event is the first annual, we don't actually know if anyone will show up. If there is a bigger race taking place elsewhere in the country on the same weekend, it may draw all the Pro and Elite teams away from Yourtown. USAC doesn't control where the best riders race, nor do they strictly coordinate the race schedule. They also don't want a new event to draw competitors away from an established event on the calendar or one of their PRT or NCC events. As such, conflicts may arise when two large events appear on the calendar on the same date, thus forcing teams to choose one over the other.

This baffles a lot of people who think that USAC plays a larger role in the organizing and scheduling of events. USA Cycling is not directly involved in the organizing or promotion of events or the establishment of teams. It has no hand in attracting sponsors to the sport, other than those that support the national team project. Its role and mission is simply "to develop the sport of cycling in the United States at all levels and to achieve sustained international racing success while fostering a shared commitment to safety, integrity, and the joy of cycling." For years, its sole function was to identify and develop riders to reach the Olympic and WorldTour levels. In recent years, it has broadened its approach to include events geared toward enthusiasts, such as gran fondos and fun rides.

There is very little guidance given to a new promoter in, say, Yourtown. The only requirement placed on promoters is that they be affiliated with a registered USAC club and have a pulse. USAC makes no concerted effort to recruit or reward race promoters. As such, the entire sport exists on the goodness of people stepping forth, taking the initiative, and often just winging it.

USAC has a training program to educate promoters on event management. At times, training and certification has been compulsory and at other times voluntary.

ANY PROMOTERS WISHING to arm themselves with market research data will be disappointed to learn that there is no central resource from which to draw such data. USAC doesn't involve itself with finding sponsors for race events or teams. It is neither a collector of, nor a repository for, demographic information. Very little market research exists to support a sponsorship search. While the bicycle industry keeps tabs on what types of bikes are being sold to what sort of consumer, there is little to no intel on who is attending a bike race or watching it online. It is, therefore, nearly impossible to educate a prospective sponsor on the potential audience that will see its logo at a bike race.

This is often misunderstood by members of the cycling community, who feel that a governing body should oversee every aspect of the sport to ensure uniformity, consistency, and vibrancy. As a result of this misunderstanding, USAC often receives sharp criticism when the sport shows signs of decline. When events disappear from the calendar or when pro teams go belly up, USAC catches heat. When sponsors pull out of the sport, fingers often point at USAC first for not having done more to stop it, when in reality, most races and teams disappear due to local influences.

A large gap exists between where USAC's role ends and a promoter's role begins. As such, the road race and criterium calendar is a mixed bag of events scattered across a very large country from March to October. USAC can't dictate which teams go to which events, nor can it always control how many national criterium races, stage races, or road races there will be. Through a selection process, it establishes a national calendar of events each year that consists of a mix of approximately 20 road races, criteriums, and stage races. It has been identified using a variety of names: National Race Calendar (NRC) and National Criterium Calendar (NCC), and more recently, the Pro Road Tour (PRT) and NRC.

The intent of the PRT is to provide a season-long series of events produced at a high standard with sizable prize lists to showcase the best national talent. In a perfect world, USAC would be able to create a perfectly balanced schedule following a convenient circuit while appealing to all types of racers. In reality, it makes the best of the events they have to work with. For example, the Yourt, also known as Picklefest. Also known as the pickle race.

USAC has outlined another series of events known as the American Road Calendar (ARC), a collection of races that are smaller in stature than the PRT. They attract many of the same teams and riders as the PRT, and they may have the same look and feel as the PRT events.

The only real distinction between the two is the separate prize lists available to the overall season winners. Since the prize list for the PRT is larger and the events are believed to have higher status, team managers like Frey give first consideration to PRT events when making out their season schedule. USAC attempts to prevent the two calendars from conflicting, but that's not an easy task.

A national calendar provides some continuity for teams racing nationally, but it poses challenges to smaller teams as it traverses the country in no convenient pattern. Follow the path of the 2017 PRT, which went west from Alabama to New Mexico to California, jumped east to North Carolina, turned back to Tulsa, and then went up to Minnesota, out to Oregon, and eventually back to New York.

For low-budget teams like Astellas, it's a huge challenge to compete for the overall series title because their budget can't cover all that ground. And a series that traversed the country in a logical pattern would still be an expensive venture for teams who have to find housing between events. Compare the US scene with that of Belgium and the

Netherlands, which have large races happening almost every other day all within an area the size of Indiana.

USAC cannot force race directors to apply for PRT or ARC status for their events, nor can they dictate upon which weekend a particular event falls, but it will often encourage them to submit an application to join one of the national calendars. Being placed on the national race calendar, it is believed, will enhance the attendance, exposure, and prestige of the event.

Joining the PRT doesn't guarantee attendance by all the biggest names in cycling. If the Pickle Festival falls on the same weekend as an ASCO conference, the Astellas team would find itself in a pickle.

AN ADDITIONAL INCENTIVE that riders have to consider when choosing which races to attend, one that transcends prize money, is the awarding of UCI points to top placings at certain high-profile events. The worldwide governing body, UCI, has an established ranking structure for events that, in turn, affects the worldwide ranking of riders. For example, more weight is given to the winner of, say, the Tour de France than the winner of the Amgen Tour of California. The winner of Paris–Roubaix is awarded more UCI points than, say, the winner of the Winston-Salem Cycling Classic. And the winner of the Larry H. Miller Tour of Utah receives more UCI points than the winner of the Cascade Cycling Classic in Bend, Oregon.

Additionally, the UCI ranking for each event dictates which type of teams will participate: WorldTour teams, Pro Continental teams, Continental teams, national teams, or any combination thereof.

Once an event reaches a certain level of popularity or status, it can campaign to be included in the UCI's race calendar, which raises the stakes considerably. The fee is higher. The event requirements are more stringent. The prize list is greater. The rules governing the race itself are more extensive. The potential to have big-name stars increases dramatically.

Sadly, by virtue of being a criterium format, Yourtown's race will never be included in the UCI's WorldTour calendar. The UCI only accepts road races and stage races in its exclusive club. And it only accepts the criterium format when it's included in a stage race. It's the equivalent of putting carrots in a chocolate cake to get kids to eat vegetables. For example, the Joe Martin Stage Race in Arkansas consists of three road races and one criterium, and it is ranked as a 2.2 event by the UCI.

There is a caveat, of course, just to make things a little more complicated. The UCI has something called an "inscripted" race, which a criterium like the Yourtown Criterium can aspire to become. In simple terms, it means that the UCI has given its blessing of sorts to a smaller race in order to allow UCI-licensed teams to compete. No UCI points are awarded in the UCI-inscripted category.

THE CONFUSION AMONG the various event rankings and UCI point structure affects only the teams, riders, and promoters. Casual fans wouldn't even know that the ranking folderol exists, nor would they have any inkling that USAC's Pro Road Tour and American Road Calendar exist when they attend a bike race. They usually make the assumption that the famous names race in the Tour de France and the not-so-famous riders race in the Yourtown Crit.

The ranking structure is not responsible for preventing the sport of cycling from becoming as popular in the United States as other pro sports. Cycling's plight can be attributed to the fact that no one has figured out how to monetize the sport. Bike races are free to the public, so there is virtually no source of revenue—ticket sales, merchandising, TV contracts, and so on. Sponsorship and entry fees are the sole revenue generators. Furthermore, the complexity of cycling makes it difficult for the common viewer to understand and appreciate the sport, so crowds are thin and sponsors shy away. And since there is no mechanism for funding other than sponsorship, teams must nurture the precarious and tenuous relationships with sponsors or angel donors to survive.

Attempts have been made to change the landscape. The National Cycle League (NCL) was a short-lived attempt at creating a major league circuit involving city-based teams competing in points-based criteriums (it lasted from 1989 to 1995). Teams with names such as the Boston Banshees, Pittsburgh Power, and Portland Thunder once roamed the earth and were owned by wealthy investors who had been sold a franchise staffed with pro and elite riders contracted to race a handful of NCL events over the course of a season. Three teams would meet in a host city, such as Tulsa, for an hour-long bike race. Five riders per team would race a points race on a short criterium course. Substitutions were allowed while the race was under way in a tag-team format using a Madison hand sling. Aggressive riding was encouraged, and at times it bordered on the theatrical in hopes of attracting viewers.

During the National Cycle League's peak in 1994, a television contract on ESPN's then brand-new channel, ESPN2, brought some attention to the sport, though attendance at races remained ridiculously low. In order to artificially hype the events, it was common among league officials to describe the crowds as numbering between 10 and 20,000 people, a statement that was completely true and wildly misleading: a crowd consisting of 28 people is, technically, more than 10. Unfortunately, the sponsors never bought the ruse and stayed away in droves.

The NCL folded when it, too, realized there was no way to monetize the sport. The seven or eight people who were watching the races on ESPN2 weren't enough to entice more sponsors to join the party.

NASCAR is usually the example given of the sponsorship model succeeding. Loyal fans follow their teams and buy the products whose logos are plastered across the hood of the car. Every weekend the stands are filled with fans paying hundreds of dollars for the opportunity to have their senses bombarded. The PGA is another popular

example of a sport that enjoys a loyal following, huge television contracts, gate revenue, and incredible sponsorship involvement. Both the
PGA and NASCAR are able to sell tickets, merchandise, and TV rights.
Both sports, while challenging and demanding of the participants, are
rather easy to understand. Cycling is not.

The PGA and NASCAR have been successful for several decades.
However, as tastes and viewing habits change, both are experiencing a
decline in numbers. Attendance has trended downward. TV viewership
dropped approximately 30 percent from 2012 to 2016 and continued
downward in 2017. With an ever-shortening attention span, viewers are
no longer willing to commit large amounts of time to watching a three-
hour telecast. Faithful Tour de France viewers will gladly sit through
six hours of a pack rolling along at 23 mph, but the general public would
rather clean their gutters than sit through a flat stage of the Tour.

JUST AS THE YOURTOWN CRIT can arise out of thin air, so can cycling teams.
There is no application to fill out for the formation of elite teams like
Astellas. No waiting list. No interview. Just a few online courses and a
background check.

There is no recruitment of team directors by USAC. In many
respects, the stone soup that is cycling exists strictly by luck. It was
entirely by chance that Matt Curin and Andrew Frey stepped forward
and started a team, just as it was entirely by chance that the promoters of the Detroit Cycling Championships had the idea to bring a race
to the Motor City. There was no application process and no interview.
The initiative started at the grassroots level.

With the right paperwork, anyone can do this anywhere, anytime.
But because there is no way to monetize a team, there are no fortunes
to be made.

Events like the Yourt will cost at least $50,000 to produce at the
lowest level. A good single-day race like the Detroit Cycling Championship costs over $200,000. Add another $50,000 for a livestream

component. A team like Astellas requires about $500,000 to run at the Continental professional level. Neither events nor teams have a way to make money—only to spend it. It's a common joke within the sport: If you want to make a million dollars, start with ten million.

ANOTHER MAJOR PROBLEM that American cycling faces, and one for which USAC catches an unfair amount of scorn, is the split personality of the sport. Here in the United States, we have long, hilly road races that roll across the countryside, and we have short, technical criteriums that closely resemble Formula One racing. Road races are like a game of Monopoly that takes a long time to play out strategically. Patience and endurance are critical. Criterium races are short, multi-lap affairs over a closed, short, technical course that last an hour or so. While they aren't unique to the United States, they're much more prevalent.

In Europe, the closest thing they have to a criterium is a kermesse, which is usually held on a 3- to 5-mile course. In America, that is called a circuit race, which falls somewhere between a road race and a crit. These crits and circuit races appeal to people with shorter attention spans. In addition, crits are much more popular among race directors in the United States because they are logistically easier to organize.

These two styles of racing—road races and criteriums—are almost two different sports entirely. They require different skill sets, draw different personalities, and divide the racing community equally. Riders who favor 120-mile road races tend to avoid criteriums, and vice versa. Road racers feel that a criterium is too dangerous and too aggressive. Criterium racers would counter that a criterium is basically the best part of a road race with the boring preamble lopped off.

Aside from the obvious differences in the races themselves, the temperaments of the racers also differ. Crit riders display a certain intensity, a swashbuckling attitude. Perhaps it's because their race tactics play out faster or because their type of racing is somehow riskier. Road racers tend to be more laid back and reserved, as if they need to conserve their energy for the next six-hour race. Not all are that way, of course, but if you entered a room with 100 bike racers, it would be pretty easy to spot the crit specialists.

Since USAC's mission is to "achieve sustained international racing success," they focus on the type of racing that is found on the international stage: road racing. There are no criteriums in the Olympics or on the UCI WorldTour, so historically USAC is most invested in developing road racers, sometimes at the expense of crits.

Many would point to the failure to exploit the popularity and charm of criterium racing as a missed opportunity. Just as there are riders who favor crits over road races, there are cycling fans who also prefer watching a criterium, either live or online. With more exposure, that audience would surely grow. Riders from other countries have come to the United States simply because they prefer the short, intense, technical rush of criteriums. Fan favorites Karl Menzies and Clay Murfet moved to the States from Tasmania specifically to race criteriums.

There are promoters in the United States who have attempted to capitalize on the popularity of criterium racing by banding together to form their own race series using only the criterium format. Speed Week and USA Crits are collections of independent races that pool their marketing efforts. They award jerseys to the overall series leader and to stage winners and offer a prize to the overall winner. And since each race is independently owned, each one is able to submit applications to be included in USAC's Pro Road Tour. There's nothing preventing them from being in both. Tour of America's Dairyland is an independent, stand-alone criterium series whose individual races have appeared on USAC's NRC and NCC calendars in the past.

Cycling's split personality makes rider development difficult when riders wish to commit to one format of racing. They will find it nearly impossible to specialize because the cost to travel to only, say, road races will be prohibitive. Finding a team that specializes in just one format is equally difficult for the same reason. It's hard to justify driving three days across the United States to race in a 90-minute criterium. Conversely, it's also hard to drive cross-country to a road race when the Yourt is an hour from your house.

Frey and Curin struggled with this problem for the first two years. Having riders like Dan Harm, who wanted to focus only on road races, limited their options when it came time to select a team to send to TOAD. (To his credit, Harm eventually came to enjoy criteriums, something he never dreamed possible.)

Embarking on its third year in 2014, the Astellas team followed the lead of other successful teams and created two squads, one to focus on criteriums and the other to focus on road races and stage races. They presumed this would make it easier to create a schedule. Rather than fight cycling's dual personality, they would design a roster that embraced it.

Their long-range goal included the addition of a women's contingent. But they would first need to prove they had the ability to operate a men's team at the Continental level.

CHAPTER 11

THE WEIGHT OF A PRO LICENSE

Though it caused a few sleepless nights, the decision to turn professional was relatively easy. Based on the success of the 2013 campaign and the experience gained over the busy summer months, Curin and Frey felt they were ready for the next challenge. Years ago their initial daydreams might have included a trip to France in a team bus so large it could blot out the sun, but since starting the team it had been their intention to rise to the Continental level, where the most rider development took place. They were both committed to their respective families and careers and knew that anything beyond that would require far too much time and energy. The riders who stayed on agreed. While the Tour de France was out of range, Curin and Frey were vying for an invitation to the Amgen Tour of California and other Medalist events.

Based in Peachtree City, Georgia, Medalist Sports is the big player in American cycling event production, responsible for putting on the Dodge Tour de Georgia, the Tour of Missouri, the Larry H. Miller Tour of Utah, the Tour of Alberta, and, for the first ten years of its existence, the Amgen Tour of California. Their events are every bit as polished and elaborate as their European counterparts. Their production values rival those of the Tour de France and even the Olympics. Utilizing a staff of 400 highly trained and experienced workers, many of whom have been with the company since the Coors Classic in the 1980s, Medalist is the gold standard for event production in the States.

For the first time since the Tour DuPont ended in 1996, someone had taken the lead in producing large-scale, multiday professional stage races in the US featuring WorldTour teams. Established by key personnel from the Tour DuPont organization, Medalist changed the landscape of cycling in the United States. By providing live TV coverage of the final two hours of each stage, Medalist's platform provided unprecedented exposure to every team. Suddenly, US-based Pro Continental and Continental teams who aspired to be included in Medalist races needed to shape their programs to fit. This meant placing an emphasis on road racing over criterium racing. Screen time in a road race was something that sponsors could understand.

Throughout the 1990s, criterium racing had become the more dominant of the two disciplines by default. Even the Coors Classic stage race in the 1980s contained some wildly popular criterium venues such as Boulder Park, Vail, and Denver's Tivoli Brewery. Pro teams traversing the country in that era made the bulk of their money by racing cash-rich criteriums. Season-long series such as the Subaru Series, the Wheat Thins Mayor's Cup, and the Saturn Cycling Series paid the riders well and drew riders from around the country. Although a road specialist named Greg LeMond was the only American to win the Tour de France, the biggest stars in the United States were at that time criterium specialists like Davis Phinney, Jonas Carney, Roberto Gaggioli, and the McCormack brothers (both sets: Paul and Alan; Mark and Frank). Almost every team in the 1980s and 1990s was geared to compete in criteriums over road races.

When Medalist began televising its stage races, starting with the Tour de Georgia in 2003, the pendulum swung back to road racing, much to the detriment of criteriums.

Personally, Curin and Frey preferred criterium racing. They were weaned on crits at Superweek and the Tour of Ohio throughout the

1990s, and they loved the excitement the race format generated and the scene in general. From a director's standpoint, crits are easier to manage because the director can simply walk around the course and shout instructions from the curb. Criteriums require significantly less equipment than a stage race. And the best part: They're over and done with in 90 minutes.

Though they hoped to someday take a contingent to the Amgen Tour, for the time being it was a distant daydream. Curin and Frey weren't about to put all their eggs in the road-racing basket, however tempting it might be. The circus atmosphere that surrounds World-Tour races is major league. A full caravan of support cars. VIP areas. Fully closed roads with enormous police support. Worldwide media covering every angle. Helicopters hovering over the peloton. It's intoxicating . . . and expensive.

Gearing up for Medalist events like the Amgen Tour or the Larry H. Miller Tour of Utah would require a budget much larger than what Curin and Frey had wrangled from Astellas thus far, and a more accomplished roster. They would need to rent a bus or RV, rent another team car, hire more staff, pay an activation fee, and bolster the organization on all levels on the outside chance that they might be one of a handful of Continental teams invited. To get the golden ticket, they would have to skew their roster toward dedicated road racers and climbers.

It was unachievable in the first year of professional status even though the team was making good progress. Plenty of teams had spent the family fortune hoping to get Medalist to look their way, only to fall short. Curin and Frey chose to keep both feet firmly on the ground.

Building a roster weighted toward road races also didn't appeal to Frey. He liked the idea of having two distinct squads, one to handle criteriums and the other to concentrate on road races as the United Healthcare team had done successfully in previous seasons.

The first new rider that Frey brought onto the team was a Belgian. Brecht Dhaene had quite a résumé, which included a year riding for the Belgian Lotto U23 team and two years with VL Technics-Abutriek. He came to the United States looking for experiences that would set him apart from his Belgian counterparts. He had been racing for 13 years already and brought with him a different set of racing sensibilities and a European discipline that American riders hadn't seen before. The American riders first saw him as odd, but quickly realized that his methods worked. While he didn't have a leadership role, he had a lot to teach the team.

Frey was happy to acquire Tasmanian Clay Murfet for the road squad. Murfet had been racing in the United States since 2006, when he came over as a junior to race on the velodrome in Trexlertown, Pennsylvania. He transitioned to road racing and joined the Kelly Benefits team as a full-fledged roadie. In the previous season Murfet had raced the full NRC schedule for the SmartStop team, including the Tour of Alberta. Frey felt he would bring large-event experience to the road squad.

Chris Uberti was a rider that the team frequently saw at midwestern races. A former teammate of Aitcheson's on the Panther team, Uberti was a solid rider and a good teammate who could also win races, as he had done in Mt. Pleasant two years earlier.

Frey's friend, David Wenger, made another recommendation. He had coached Michael Pincus personally since 2008 and liked his trajectory. He had an upbeat attitude and analytical mind that he applied to cycling as well as to his studies in electrical engineering at the University of Houston. A quick phone call to Frey was all it took to find him a team for the upcoming season.

The addition of Andy Baker delivered more experience to the team. He was with the Bissell cycling team when they won the NRC overall title. His résumé also included two years with the Hincapie development team and a win at the Division II collegiate national championship road race in 2011 while at Furman University.

Stephen Hyde was an up-and-coming cyclocross racer from Massachusetts who also excelled on the road. He had ridden well at road

nationals the previous year. He was a strong all-rounder who was looking to build speed into his preparation for the cyclocross season, which
follows the road racing season by about four minutes. Hyde knew that
racing on the road would make him faster off it.

Hogan Sills was invited back onto the team. He had ridden for the
Astellas Oncology team as a Category II rider in 2012, but was left off
the team in 2013 when the team limited itself to just Category I riders.
He was a solid rider with a strong sprint.

Justin Williams was another great addition, coming off a year on
the Rock Racing team and the Trek-Livestrong team. Armed with a big
smile and an outgoing personality, he brought positive energy to the
criterium squad, along with a fast sprint. He and Hyde were both adept
storytellers who had the ability to make a four-hour van ride feel like
10 minutes.

NOW THAT THEY WERE CALLING IT a professional cycling team, Curin and Frey
thought they might have an easier time finding endemic sponsors.
Surprisingly, they ran into the same buzz saw of rejection that they
experienced as a Domestic Elite team in 2012 and 2013. They used every
connection they could to establish any sort of relationship with equipment manufacturers. They called every phone number on every card
collected at Interbike, the industry's annual trade show in Las Vegas,
hoping to procure equipment for the new season. The only vendor
sticking around for another year was clothing manufacturer Pactimo,
but Astellas would need more than just clothing. They were also hoping to find a bike supplier.

Based on a tip from Frankie Andreu, who knew how the winds blow
through the bike industry, they sent sponsorship proposals to a handful of popular bike manufacturers, hoping to avoid having to purchase
their bikes as they had in the first two seasons. Litespeed was at the top
of their list. Absent from the pro cycling scene for a number of years,
Litespeed was, indeed, looking for a team to support.

A well-respected bike manufacturer famous for high-end titanium frames, Litespeed was now making carbon fiber frames. They had sponsored the Lotto-Adecco team in 2002, but were, in essence, driven out of the team sponsorship game when the price for entry became cost-prohibitive for specialty companies. By 2014, with the national championships taking place in their hometown of Chattanooga, they were looking for an affordable sponsorship project that would carry their brand in high-profile races without breaking the bank.

Two teams had submitted sponsorship requests to Litespeed in 2014: Astellas and a well-established team based on the East Coast. The other team had requested much more matériel: two road bikes and a time trial bike for every rider on the team, plus an additional stable of frames to use as spares, which was not an uncommon request. Frey had requested a modest number of bike frames, just enough to provide each rider with one frame and a few extras to use as spares.

Based on cost alone, Astellas's request was far more attractive. Bike-industry sponsorships at this level are, at best, charity. Sales of Litespeed or any other manufacturer's bikes barely see an uptick thanks to a Continental team's involvement. The best Litespeed could hope for was a little exposure at races as a reminder to consumers that they were still in the game.

With a new three-year contract signed, Astellas's riders would be on Litespeed's carbon fiber bikes through the 2016 season. It was a big get for the team.

The team continued to piggyback on the United Airlines corporate account through Astellas. Same with hotels, though they switched from the Hyatt account to Marriott. Rudy Project gave them another box of sunglasses. Otherwise, there weren't a lot of logos cluttering up the jersey.

They would make do with what they had. The bills were paid. That's all that really mattered.

CHAPTER 12

SEASON 3: PINK, GRAY, AND WHITE

Expectations were low going into the team's first season as a professional squad. Racing against the Continental pro teams meant Astellas would be starting at the bottom of a bigger food chain.

The purchase of a new Mercedes Sprinter van raised their profile. Wrapped in sponsors' logos, it made quite an impression when it pulled into the team parking area. But more than looking the part, teams are judged on one thing: their ability to race bikes. Win or lose, the Astellas team needed to be willing to work and prepared to suffer. A sponsor's reputation or bank account doesn't win respect from the peloton. In fact, having a big sponsor only piles on the pressure.

In their debut at San Dimas and Redlands, the first events on USAC's National Road Calendar, the team's efforts fell short of their own expectations. No one was able to crack the top 25 at San Dimas. Jake Rytlewski and Cortlan Brown were the best finishers at Redlands in 25th and 33rd places, while Korus finished in sixth place for the sprinter's jersey, but down in the overall standings. Andy Baker's bike broke at both events, which left him frustrated. Despite all that, Dhaene, Uberti, Green, Baker, Korus, Aitcheson, and Thomas Brown, a late addition that Murfet brought with him from SmartStop, were starting to gel as teammates when they showed up to race in North Carolina two weeks later.

Winston-Salem has a decent cycling scene and has played host to great races in the past. The inaugural Winston-Salem Cycling Classic included a 170 km hilly road race in and around Winston-Salem on Saturday and a 90-minute criterium downtown on Sunday.

There were 180 riders at the race start, nearly outnumbering the spectators. Even at the pro level, national level races are poorly attended despite the work that is put into promoting the event. It's easy to question why people go to the trouble of putting on bike races. In fact, races exist because people ignore that question.

With a good-sized field, there was plenty of horsepower to drive the pace, and a crowd of candidates jockeyed to make it into the breakaway. Baker, now sporting a fully operational bike, was one of the early attackers to be reeled in. Shortly after the halfway point, a three-man breakaway formed. Green established a lead with Oscar Clark from United Healthcare and David Cueli from the regional United Healthcare of Georgia team, only to be eventually caught by a chase group comprised of all the pre-race favorites. Green dropped out of the lead group, but Dhaene came across the gap with a few other riders, putting Astellas in the breakaway for the rest of the race and finishing in 11th place. Meanwhile, the field had been sawed in half by the hard pace. Only 80 starters would be permitted to ride Sunday's criterium.

On the heels of the punishing 170 km road race, a 90-minute criterium seemed like an easy sprint. A large crowd made it fun, cheering at the right times and staying until the end. This is what brings the teams to town.

As for criterium racing, the United Healthcare and Optum–Kelly Benefits teams were the kings of the craft. The United Healthcare team had a penchant for lining up six riders at the front of the field in the final laps of a race and taking control of the pace, earning them the nickname "Blue Train." When the heat was on, Optum–Kelly Benefits was sure to unleash its notorious sprinters. Both teams affected the outcome of every race they entered.

If a rider could manage to get into a breakaway with members of those two teams, he was assured of some sort of success because any chase effort would be shut down with authority. Without either of those two teams represented in a breakaway, the riders could count on being reeled in like mackerel before reaching the finish line, their hopes dashed in a blur of blue or orange.

The Astellas team was weighing its options pre-race and grappling with a real disadvantage—they didn't really know what they were capable of yet. Thomas Brown had the most crit experience, having spent time on the SmartStop team a year earlier and having raced against many of these riders. He felt he was the obvious choice to be the protected rider. Six of the seven Astellas riders went to the line with the same thought in mind, but ultimately the race would decide the team leader.

The lone dissenter was Aitcheson. He went to the line with bigger issues on his mind. Two laps into the race, his teammates caught a glimpse of him standing on the sidewalk doubled over in gastric distress. He had been complaining of food poisoning symptoms prior to the start and considered skipping the race completely. Each time the peloton passed by, his teammates noticed he was a different shade of green.

After 25 minutes of racing, Cueli made an attack that was joined by Canadian Remi Peletier-Roy of the Garneau-Quebecor team. When the two established a 10-second lead, Astellas's Brecht Dhaene bridged across to them. He knew there was almost no chance they would make it to the finish without United Healthcare or Optum represented, but still he instinctively chased it down.

As soon as he made contact with the leaders, Dhaene settled into a rotation in which all three riders shared the load evenly. For several laps they dangled out in front of the field with a 12-second lead, but it wasn't a lead to take seriously. The peloton seemed to toy with the breakaway, letting them burn themselves up going nowhere. At times, the gap shrank to nine seconds, but there was still daylight between the two groups.

Over the next 10 laps, the lead grew to 20 seconds and then reached its largest margin of 23 seconds with 20 minutes of racing remaining.

In the minds of everyone standing along the course, it was just a matter of time before the Blue Train fired up the engines and began to pick up the pace. Even the race announcers, Richard Fries and Chad Andrews, treated it as a foregone conclusion. They had seen it happen countless times, and 23 seconds wasn't an insurmountable gap. The field never lost sight of the breakaway. Had the gap grown large enough, the breakaway could have ducked around a corner and out of sight of the chasers. Once out of sight, they could slip out of mind. But the field never took their eyes off the breakaway.

With five laps to go, Uberti went to the front of the field to disrupt the chase efforts, which may have bought Dhaene a few extra seconds. Thomas Brown followed suit, attentive to any last-minute attacks. If the Blue Train was about to roll, he was determined to be on board.

With four laps to go, the lead was holding at a mere 20 seconds.

Two laps later, the Blue Train had cut the lead to 10 seconds. Dhaene and the other two riders in the breakaway looked visibly tired. They began to waggle back and forth, trying to find fresh muscles. There were none to be found. Their lead was vanishing rapidly.

If the breakaway riders hesitated for an instant to jockey for position, the Blue Train would roll over them. They would need to hold their speed all the way to the end in order to have a chance, but they had been off the front for more than an hour, and it showed. Their heads hung low. Their shoulders were hunched up.

The bell rang, signaling one lap to go. The breakaway was just 50 meters in front of a hard-charging peloton now led by the orange-clad Optum–Kelly Benefits team, who clearly smelled blood in the water.

Reaching speeds of 45 mph on the downhill on the backstretch, the trio held on to a three-bike-length gap. Less than 20 feet.

With just a few corners left to negotiate, the last bit of daylight separating the two groups disappeared. The last rider in the break was caught, but Dhaene accelerated into the final turns with one last effort. As he flew through the final corner, his legs started to cramp. Luckily for Dhaene, the final turn was just 62 meters from the finish line. Had it been 72 meters, he would have finished in third place. Instead, he won.

Astellas celebrated up and down the home stretch and at home in Milwaukee. The other teams were in a state of shock, left to wonder about this team in pink and gray.

In a post-race interview Daniel Holloway, a pre-race favorite riding for the small Domestic Elite team Athlete Octane Cycling, said that the field "got awfully close. He didn't win by much." He didn't need to.

Astellas gained legitimacy with the win. The relative anonymity that Dhaene had benefited from going into that race was a thing of the past. The foreigner that no one knew, riding for the team that they only kind of knew, won one of the bigger races.

When it came time for the prize money to be distributed, there was a kerfuffle over who contributed what to the cause and when. Once things settled down, the guys realized it was nice to be able to argue over a race purse. Even the teammates who didn't race the criterium in Winston-Salem felt a deep sense of pride as they watched the road squad come back from losing the road race and go on to win the criterium. The early-season win galvanized the team.

AITCHESON SPENT THE NEXT WEEK down for the count with a full case of food poisoning. A few weeks later he accompanied the team to Silver City, New Mexico, for the Tour of the Gila, but he never left the hotel room.

Still riding high after Dhaene's win, the team felt they could contend at Gila, if not for the overall, then at least for a stage win. They rolled into town in good spirits.

As the caravan vehicles lined up at the starting line before the first stage, a single ambulance assumed its customary position at the back of the line as a precaution if any riders crashed heavily and needed advanced medical treatment.

The stage was 90 miles, finishing with a 7-mile climb on Mogollon Road that featured 19 percent grades through the Gila National Forest, a rugged landscape of mountains, canyons, and all sorts of wildlife.

Korus found his way into a breakaway group of four that included Astellas alum Hartrich, who had found a new team in the off-season. Their lead peaked at 10 minutes before the field became motivated to begin chasing. Aided by a tailwind and a slight but straight downhill terrain, the pack flew down the road at 50 mph with teams fighting to hit the final climb at the front. All the teams were following in the draft of United Healthcare's Blue Train when two UHC riders touched wheels and a cascade of bikes and bodies ensued.

Eighty riders went down. Only 20 made it past the crash unscathed. Several riders were caught behind the pile, which completely blocked the road. Team directors and mechanics jumped out of the following team cars and ran to find their riders. Amid the chaos, they tried to assess which riders needed medical attention and which ones could continue the race.

The entire Astellas team fell in the same heap. They had been riding in tight formation behind the Blue Train when the crash unfolded. In just seconds bodies went skidding across the rough road surface, bikes and bike parts tumbled in every direction, and sunglasses and Garmins catapulted into the air. (In the days following the crash, the local bike shop collected 20 wayward Garmin units.)

Cortlan face-planted into the back of another rider and was then buried under several bodies and bikes. Unable to free himself, he could hear other riders screaming for a medic as he assessed his own injuries.

Of the Astellas riders, only Green got up to finish the stage. The rest of the team was messed up. The intense New Mexico sun had cooked the surface of the pavement into a coarse sandpaper-like surface, which caused incredible damage to everyone and everything.

Several riders did not continue the stage, and more withdrew from the race the next day. Some were transported by team car to the hospital in Silver City. Two riders from the Silber team were airlifted to El Paso 150 miles away, only to have the same strong winds that pushed the speed of the race force the helicopter to divert to Tucson instead.

Every bit of the Astellas equipment was destroyed. Skinsuits, helmets, shoes, bikes, wheels, glasses, and derailleurs were either shattered or scraped by the rough pavement. In the days that followed, the riders attempted to tally up the retail cost of the equipment ruined in the crash and stopped when they reached $100,000.

The local surgeon had been racing in the Category III race when the crash occurred and had to be pulled from the race and driven to the hospital, which was overrun with cyclists. Dhaene Brecht broke a collarbone. Cortlan required surgery on his knee. Baker flew home the same night covered in gauze, only to later develop a methicillin-resistant staphylococcus aureus (MRSA) infection in his knee that landed him in the hospital for a week. Disheartened and equally fed up and burned out, he retired from the sport soon after. It wasn't how he wanted his cycling career to end, but he had no interest in changing the script.

The next day, Green and Korus were involved in another high-speed crash in which Korus broke his collarbone. Green was battered badly. Now the entire team was out of the race. It took $15,000 to get the team to Gila, and they were decimated in the first two days.

There were very few lessons to be learned from the carnage. A crash that intense is a fluke. Every rider knows it's part of cycling. For some, it took a while to get the crash out of their heads, but eventually they moved on. The only other option was to quit the sport.

WHILE THE ROAD SQUAD was dealing with the crash at Gila, the crit squad was racing at the mother of all twilight criteriums in Georgia.

Celebrating 35 years in 2014, Athens Twilight was, and is, one of the most popular and longest-running criteriums in the country. Held within stumbling distance of the University of Georgia campus and its 34,000-strong student body, Twilight draws thousands of college students out of the bars on Clayton Street each year hoping to see something insane. The UGA students who witnessed the first Twilight in 1980 are now approaching retirement age, and some still attend the race.

The event touts its reputation for producing memorable crashes. Anything that can happen in a criterium has happened at Twilight: disqualifications, neutralizations, relegations, hospitalizations, altercations, public urinations, and wedding proposals. Racers simultaneously love and hate it, but they return every year because of the party atmosphere and the insanity of racing in the dark at 30 mph, and because it's Twilight.

About halfway through the race, with a two-man breakaway holding a 20-second lead and two riders in the gap, the peloton filed through the first turn at 28 mph. The rider on the front, Emile Abraham, crashed into the barricades, causing about 10 riders to pile up. The rest of the field squeezed by and accelerated back up to speed. Moments later, the race official following the field on a motorcycle stopped to aid the fallen riders, including Abraham, who wasn't moving. He positioned his motorcycle to protect the riders, but it was also at the exit apex of the turn, which meant that it blocked the preferred line of travel through the corner and couldn't be seen by riders as they entered the turn. Seconds later, the breakaway came through the turn and swerved to avoid collision. Just a few seconds behind them, the chase group of two squeezed through the turn. A couple of seconds after, the field came through again.

Uberti was the first one through, and he avoided hitting anything. A few more riders barely missed the stationary motorcycle. Several struck the motorcycle and barricades and tumbled in a ball of color and carbon. Hyde hit the rear of the motorcycle and somersaulted onto it. Sills also tumbled into the pile of riders.

Because of the short distance of each lap, it was nearly impossible for word of the crash to get back to the main officials at the start-finish line in time to warn the riders. Two more laps went by before the main pack took it upon themselves to stop the race, clear the incident, and restart.

Unfortunately, the breakaway and chase groups continued unabated and nearly lapped the field before the officials were able to stop them. The ensuing protests were numerous and took several minutes to sort out.

The post-race debates continued for weeks afterward. Everyone had an opinion as to the cause, the blame, and the best remedy to prevent something like that from happening again. Most of the racers in the race, however, simply chalked it up to the nature of the beast.

The final results weren't good for the Astellas teams. Thomas Brown was their highest finisher in 28th. A resident of Athens, he had hoped to do better in what he considered his home race. Instead, he and his teammates were lucky to have suffered no major injuries. Emile Abraham came away with a concussion, a broken nose, and a gash above his right eye that required six stitches. Had the official's motorcycle not been parked where it was, it could have been catastrophic for him.

AT THE TOUR OF AMERICA'S DAIRYLAND in June, the racing was fast, the courses were fun, and the crowds were knowledgeable. And the crit squad rode well. Monk rode with the confidence of a seasoned crit specialist. By week's end he would be in third place overall and have three top-five finishes to his name. Justin Williams was riding at his peak. He won stages in Oshkosh and Beloit, and finished second in Fond du Lac. But most of the week's fun happened on Milwaukee's Upper Eastside.

Located near the University of Wisconsin's Milwaukee campus, the race on "Downer Ave." (Avenue takes too much energy to say, so cyclists shorten it to Ave. Always.) has been a happening place in the bike-racing world since the 1980s, when it was part of the Superweek races, a series that ran for more than 40 years throughout southern

Wisconsin. There are huge crowds on the home stretch and yard parties on the back stretch. The crowd brings out the very best in the racers, and the race is always fast.

If the Downer Ave. atmosphere could be bottled and poured on other races, cycling would be the most popular sport in America. Some of the families on the backstretch have hosted criterium parties for decades. They've seen enough racing to know in seconds whether a breakaway group has the right mix to succeed. TOAD is so ingrained in the fabric of the community that when a home on the backstretch goes up for sale, the race is typically mentioned in the listing.

The winner receives a check for about $350, measly by pro sports standards. But the race itself is an American monument like the Athens Twilight and others. The winner's name is added to a who's who of past winners.

Meanwhile, just around the corner from the finish line, there is another stripe painted across the road to mark the location of the Super Prime. Since 2005, Ben's Cycles bike shop in Milwaukee has put together a huge party on the course and raises $5,000 by selling brats, beer, and T-shirts. The money is awarded to the winner of a lap of their choosing. The local bike shop spectacle is completely independent of the race itself, and the racers love it too, adding to the delight of the Downer Ave. crowd. The $5,000 purse exceeds the annual salary of most Conti pro riders. It is also more than a rider would receive for winning every single stage of TOAD.

The first half of the race was uneventful for the Astellas team. They had missed a couple of breakaway attempts and had to help reel them in. Like every other elite cyclist, they were familiar with the Super Prime and felt they had a contender in Williams. They were content to ride the entire race for the Super Prime lap.

The bell rang out sometime in the latter part of the race, when riders were tired. The Astellas team responded, lining up at the front of the field and drilling the pace with Williams sitting in the catbird's seat. Everyone else saw the move and hopped on board.

The racecourse is shaped like a four-cornered triangle, which may sound geometrically impossible, but the last two corners are so close together that the field makes one big sweeping arc through them. The finishing straightaway is about 400 meters long, and the Super Prime line is only about 120 meters beyond the first turn. The sprint was a drag race down the long straightaway led by the last couple of Astellas lead-out riders. Green peeled off, Hyde, and then Murfet. Whoever hit the turn first would have the advantage. Williams was the first into the turn, and three riders came sprinting out of it—Rahsaan Bahati, Holloway, and Williams.

Justin Williams won the Super Prime and the biggest payday of the year for the fledgling crit squad by just a couple of inches.

AMERICAN BIKE RACES like Downer Ave. are awesome, but Belgium is cycling's promised land. In August, a trip to cycling's Mecca was made possible thanks to the concerted effort of Dhaene and Green. They caught a glimpse of Frey's world as they secured housing, booked flights, registered for races, and mapped out a schedule. Uberti, Pincus, Korus, Cortlan Brown, Murfet, Green, and Dhaene loaded up as much as they could carry through an airport and headed to Belgium to race.

They rented a house in the country just far enough from town to make things inconvenient. And with no money allotted for a rental car, they spent the month living like Capone's mob hiding out after a heist, leaving only to conduct business.

A few days into the trip, they were hit with the disheartening news from the home office that the team would not receive any more money from its sponsors for the remainder of the season. This meant the guys would need to scrimp at every turn in order to stay abroad for the entire schedule. Any luxuries or extras would be paid using their own money. It felt as if the rug had been pulled out from under them.

To add to their mood, it rained every single day for the entire month.

The house was just a short ride from most of the races, and race organizers helped by providing them with transportation to the distant ones. They raced a handful of UCI 1.1 and 1.2 races such as Arnhem-Veenendaal Classic, GP Stad Zottegem, and Antwerpse Havenpijl. Each race covered 190 kilometers on the same narrow roads and many of the cobbled climbs that make the spring classics famous.

Random stretches of Belgian road, upon which all the great riders have raced, are known to overwhelm cyclists with emotion. The area is so rich in cycling history that every hill has a name that dedicated cycling fans can recite with ease. Many of the roads are no wider than a golf cart path, and many are in far worse shape than the crummy, pothole-laden roads they ride every day back home, but to a cyclist, they are hallowed grounds ridden with reverence.

A race in Geraardsbergen took the team up the legendary Mur de Grammont several times. It was enough to give them an appreciation for just how hard the short, punchy climbs of the Ronde von Vlaanderen (Tour of Flanders) can be, but it wasn't the magical Belgian experience they had hoped for. They entire trip, in fact, felt like nothing more than a series of grueling races in the rain. The horsepower in the 180-man field was staggering. Races went all-out for four hours with an endless lineup of fresh riders finding their way to the front of the field and pushing the pace. The Astellas contingent rarely saw the Belgian countryside or appreciated the racing history of the famous roads because they were holding on for dear life with eyes glued to the wheel ahead of them. Their best result was Brecht's 33rd place at Antwerpse Havenpijl. Cortlan took 44th at the Arnhem race.

The romantic notion of gritting one's teeth and riding in the rain on storied European roads and finishing covered in grime grew hollow, but the riders were discovering a new capacity for suffering by enduring the losing battle. Even still, there was consensus that they were ready to go home to race on familiar roads. And dry off.

LEFT OFF THE BELGIUM ROSTER, Aitcheson tried to salvage his season by racing as many crits as he could before everything ground to a halt in September. He joined up with the crit squad at the Chris Thater Memorial in Binghamton, New York, and the Gateway Cup in St. Louis, Missouri. The more he raced, the faster his fitness rebounded, and the more he came to prefer 90 minutes of concentrated racing over four-hour marathons. His newfound passion for criteriums would keep him inspired through the winter months.

As a Canadian rider, he wouldn't be eligible to compete with the crit squad when they attended the US Criterium National Championships in High Point, North Carolina, in September. As it turned out, the rest of the team was eager to taper their training after a long season of racing. Only Thomas Brown and Monk showed up for the late-season national championship.

The criterium in High Point offered no highlights for the Astellas riders. Brown and Feehery missed the decisive move that saw 20 riders roll away from the field and go up the road to decide the winner among themselves.

It might have been a mistake not to require every American Astellas rider to attend the national championship events, but the dwindling funds wouldn't have covered much of the expense. Frey was in no position to insist on riders attending on their own dime.

ONE OF THE ROAD SQUAD'S final events of the 2014 season was the Bucks County Classic in Pennsylvania, which consisted of a UCI 1.2 road race followed by a downtown criterium.

Saturday's road race took place on the hills surrounding New Hope. A huge field rolled out onto a hilly 100-mile course that wore down the field with its relentless ups and downs. Rain began to fall halfway through the race, making things miserable, even for the riders who raced in Belgium. Eventually, 130 riders abandoned the race, leaving only 50 finishers to cross the line. Brecht and Cortlan were the only Astellas riders to finish. Brecht's dad had come over from Belgium to see him race, and his son mustered a sprint from the third group to finish in 10th place.

Sunday's criterium finished with a field sprint made up of 90 riders. Most of the riders who finished well in the road race the day before finished behind the crit specialists. Brecht grabbed another 10th-place finish, affirming his standing as one of the high-caliber riders in the field.

Despite the conditions and the team's attrition issue, the Bucks County race was a milestone for the riders. They had survived the season, grown as riders, and hung their hat on some great performances. They entered the off-season feeling that they had progressed as a team.

FREY AND CURIN had thought that things would somehow be easier once the team made the jump to the pro level. Surely things would take care of themselves to some extent, sort themselves out. That wasn't the case.

They had more riders to deal with. Sixteen riders divided into two groups going in different directions posed more challenges to Frey, who now had two young children of his own and another on the way. The workload nearly doubled, with twice as many events and more jockeying over who would be the designated leader at each one. It's natural for riders to expect the team to work for them at certain races and get upset when they don't get the support they feel they deserve. It's the classic dilemma: riders need results to progress upward, but they often have to take a backseat to other riders on the team.

Generally, the team didn't experience significant infighting. They learned to move as a team, each rider sharing what knowledge he could. They had Williams and Hyde to keep them entertained with endless stories of life on the road. They held court in the team van during long drives. The quick-witted Aussie, Murfet, never let the mood get too dark. They benefited from the European experience of Dhaene and Green.

They also had other teams eyeing them. In their first year of racing at the pro level, the Astellas team was getting to a lot of races and gaining great experience.

There's a culture of tough love handed down by the teams higher up the food chain. Every team has to earn its spot, but once that happens, they are in the brotherhood. It's really no different than a regular job; gaining the respect of coworkers comes first. Especially if the job involves flying down the road at 30 mph just inches away from teammates and rivals wearing nothing but an ultra-thin layer of fabric.

While the trip to Belgium was not the magical pilgrimage they had hoped for, it hardened them for the next level of bike racing. Throughout the season, Astellas had earned the respect of other teams. Their appearances at pharmaceutical events for their sponsor had all been positive. In general, their first year at the pro level had been a success.

CHAPTER 13

THE FRIENDS AND FAMILY PLAN

In the course of a single cycling season, riders experience euphoric highs and soul-crushing lows. What keeps riders from becoming manic are the people that fill in the range of emotions located between those two extremes. Without them, the season would destroy everyone before nationals. Riders are forced to be friends with their teammates; it's the other people who keep them human.

The person who is most critical in keeping riders on an even keel is the soigneur. WT and PCT teams are required to have full-time staff, so the inclusion of a soigneur is pretty standard. Conti teams aren't required to have any staff members, so it's not a guarantee that they'll hire a soigneur. If they do, it will likely be on a freelance or "as needed" basis. Astellas didn't have enough work or money to justify having a soigneur on staff, but they needed a trained massage therapist to provide massages to riders competing at multiday stage races. Whenever Deb Rawluk or Paige Alexandra showed up at a race, the riders enjoyed the added luxury of being relieved of laundry and cooking duties.

A hockey-playing, marathon-running massage therapist from Edmonton, Alberta, Deb didn't know much about cycling. She came on board for Redlands and the Grand Prix Cycliste de Saguenay, and quickly learned how to hand up bottles in the feed zone and set up the campsite in the team parking lot. Her counterpart Paige was well-versed in the cycling scene, having worked with the US National Track cycling team, Kenda/5-Hour Energy, Cylance Pro Cycling, and the Trek Factory Racing mountain bike team.

Being a soigneur requires an eclectic set of skills, a nurturing personality, and complete willingness to work outside a well-defined job description. The most important task is to help tired legs recover, but the job goes well beyond that. Soigneurs prepare and organize the food to be handed to the riders during the race. They fill the water bottles, mix the powdered sports drinks, replenish the ice, and pack it all into one cooler that rides with the team director and another one that travels to the feed zone. At the feed zone, they will hand the food and bottles to the riders passing by at 27 mph.

Heading into a weeklong event, soigneurs will easily drop $1,200 at Kroger, Albertsons, Meijer, or Food Lion. They will fill up two carts with a collection of items ranging from rice to nylons, confusing even the most seasoned checker. How the food is prepared depends on the agreed-upon tastes of the team. Bars and gels are staples, but the riders typically settle on a particular food to be handed up over the course of each season. One year it might be Hawaiian dinner rolls filled with bananas and honey, wrapped in aluminum foil. Another year, homemade rice cakes. Once the order is in, there will be those riders who approach the soigneur with their own special requests, such as waffles with Nutella or peanut butter and jelly on whole wheat.

On race day, the soigneur drives the van to the starting venue while the team rides their bikes from the hotel to the venue. The swanny arrives early to set up the team's basecamp in the team parking area and set out each rider's backpack, taking into account who likes to sit where. In hot weather, the nylons are filled with ice so they can be easily packed into riders' jerseys to keep them cool later in the day.

Once the riders head to the starting line, the soigneur repacks the van and prepares to leave for the feed zone. This effort is often interrupted by a rider who comes back to look for something that he can't live without, maybe a different pair of sunglasses with either darker or lighter lenses. Chances are good that it's buried in his backpack under 50 spare wheels and a pop-up tent.

A loosely organized caravan of team vans departs for the feed zone, hopefully led by experienced team soigneurs who remember where the feed zone was in previous years. Amateur team soigneurs desperately try to keep up with the caravan so as not to get lost, all while thinking, "This is insane," and "It's completely unnecessary to drive so fast."

The caravan arrives at the feed zone somewhere between 30 seconds and one hour before the first riders arrive and stand just meters apart from one another without speaking. They're not unfriendly; they're just too tired. After handing up the bottles and musette bags, the soigneurs drive to the finish, where they essentially do the same thing all over again.

After the race is over, it's time to return to the hotel, clean out the van, and begin massages for each rider, which take another 2.5 hours. Having eaten breakfast and lunch on the go, the soigneur will eat dinner out of a takeaway container while doing laundry.

It's a hard job on game day. Non-race days are only slightly less busy.

The soigneurs are trusted with the inner secrets of the peloton. Gripes and complaints that can't be voiced elsewhere are shared openly. If a rider is unhappy, the swanny will know it before the team director. As a rider bounces from hotel to hotel, from van to train to plane, the soigneur is the friendly face that riders look forward to seeing, showing up just in time to make things better.

ONE OF THE CHRONIC LOWS a traveling bike racer will experience throughout the season is abject boredom. And despite having teammates in their space 24/7, there is a degree of loneliness that the sport just can't shake. Only so much of the week can be filled with races. The rest is spent riding, recovering from workouts, and resting up for the next race. That usually entails watching Netflix, scrolling through Twitter, and poring over power data while sitting in a hotel room, a car, an airport, or on a plane. It's not an easy life.

In addition to the normal tedium, foreign riders find themselves thousands of miles from home. They must develop an entirely new routine in their adopted American towns. Sometimes fresh eyes and foreign sensibilities can play to a rider's advantage. For example, Milwaukee or Knoxville are hardly "garden spots" in the minds of most Americans, but these cities were all-new to the international riders who came to race for Astellas. Clay Murfet found Knoxville to be heaven on Earth. Matt Green remains unabashedly in love with Milwaukee. Both riders traveled extensively throughout the country, taking in a wide variety of American towns and landscapes. On returning to their respective cities, they explored what city life had to offer, focused on the good parts, and put down roots.

For most cyclists, the livability of a city is determined by an audit of its roads and coffee shops and whether it can sustain some semblance of a social life. Figuring out the road system is the first priority for cyclists, since that is where most of their time will be spent. Where can they ride safely, without fearing for their lives every moment they are on a bike? Where can they ride far, unimpeded by traffic lights and stop signs? Where can they access decent terrain without having to load the bike into a car to get there? Is the city bike-friendly, with well-enforced bike lanes? Is there an established bike culture? While Chicago and San Francisco rank high on *Bicycling* magazine's list of bike-friendly cities, these sprawling urban jungles require a rider to drive out of the city to find decent cycling roads. Smaller cities such as Boulder, Colorado, and Tucson, Arizona, attract riders to quiet roads that are accessible from within city limits.

A city doesn't have to have all of the accoutrements of a bike-friendly city in place in order to be friendly toward cyclists. That is, lane markings approved by the state department of transportation, infrastructure, and city ordinances. Attitudes toward cyclists vary from city to city and range from loving to hostile, and they seem to follow no sensible pattern. Experienced cyclists can usually spot the telltale signs of a friendly city within a few days of riding. Parts of Los Angeles offer great riding, while other areas are untouchable. Boulder was a bike-friendly town decades before the city committed to additional infrastructure. Detroit, Michigan, however, needed the help of city planners to overcome years of the automobile's domination.

After the road assessment comes caffeination. The quantity and quality of coffee shops can make or break a town in the mind of a cyclist. Is the coffee halfway decent? Are the shops dispersed so as to accommodate a two-hour coffee break on a long day of training? Do they roast their own blends? Are their scones baked in-house? These are valid concerns.

Coming in third on a cyclist's checklist is the prospect of a social life. Over the course of the season, cyclists will find themselves in college towns, military towns, farming towns, and suburbia. While there is little time for socializing, they are acutely aware that their peers are attempting to find love. Cyclists are no different, so they turn to the popular Tinder app when they find themselves alone in strange towns.

When Green left England to race for the Astellas team in 2013, he was merely looking to gain experience and results before returning to Europe. About a year into the adventure, he realized it wasn't as temporary as he had originally planned. The decision to continue racing with Astellas meant that his current relationship with a woman across the Atlantic was doomed. In time, he began looking for an American woman to spend time with.

Green's British accent siphons all the attention in the room, making him a horrible wingman. His wild shock of hair is hip, and his experience traveling the world makes him a natural conversationalist.

He met a few women in Milwaukee, but he found it difficult to have a relationship when he was never in the town where he supposedly lived. While some actively seek those types of relationships, Green wasn't one of them.

He turned to Tinder not because he was looking for a casual hookup but because it doesn't cost anything. That's the motivation behind a lot of decisions made by struggling athletes. Buying ramen noodles, sleeping in the car, dining out at all-you-can-eat buffets, and using the neighbor's Wi-Fi to get on free dating sites are standard. As they see it, only royalty, 1-percenters, and the fiscally inept pay $30 per month for a dating site.

A few of Green's Astellas teammates had used Tinder for hookups, and they assured him that the full range of relationships could be found on the site, so he downloaded the app onto his phone and fired it up. He swiped to the right on the very first picture that appeared on his screen: Tracy's. Tracy, who had been forced into using Tinder by well-meaning friends, also swiped right on the first face she saw on Tinder: Matt's.

The two conversed via text and phone for a few days before they finally arranged to meet at a stage of TOAD. Tracy dragged some friends to Milwaukee's Schlitz Park to watch Green race. She said nothing before or during the race to indicate that she had arrived. After the race, Green got cleaned up and dragged Michael Pincus with him for moral support, carrying him on the back of his bike so that he wouldn't have to walk—and so he couldn't escape. When they found Tracy and her friends, Tracy, without saying a word, boldly walked up to Green and put her fingers in his hair. They were a couple from that moment on. In 2016, they became engaged and a year later they were married.

Tracy became part of the Astellas family.

Clay Murfet has an almost identical story. After shattering his wrist in a crash at San Dimas, he spent several weeks recovering at a home he shared with teammate Thomas Brown in Athens, Georgia. Assured that Tinder would help him find someone to listen to his cycling stories, if only temporarily, Murfet created an account.

Minutes after launching the app, the very first photo that appeared on his phone was that of a very attractive woman named Hannah, who was studying social work and public health at the University of Georgia. He nervously swiped the screen to the right with his finger and sat at his kitchen table, anxiously staring at his phone.

Hannah also swiped right.

They met at the Allgood Lounge, a bar located on the Athens Twilight course between the final turn and the finish line. To Murfet's good fortune, Hannah noticed his quick wit and big heart.

Hannah and Murfet spent three solid days together, during which he became smitten and then hooked. When he went in for the first kiss and missed, he nearly chipped a tooth. He was that much out of practice.

Upon graduating from UGA, Hannah took a job in Knoxville, Tennessee, and Murfet followed. Two years later, they were married.

Were it not for a broken wrist sustained in a crash on the other side of the country, their romance might have never happened. The forced time off the bike gave him time to commit energy to something other than racing.

Monk's story is completely dissimilar. He didn't need Tinder, Bumble, or any other app. He met his future wife while they were in kindergarten. Lyss was his biggest fan from day one and willingly showed up at every race. Their relationship spanned several race seasons, culminating in an engagement during the 2016 season, proving that true love transcends the Pro Road Tour.

ANOTHER SOURCE OF LOVE in a bike racer's world is the strong bond that's formed with host families. A completely random connection often turns into lifelong friendship when people volunteer to let total strangers—bike racers, no less—live in their home for several days.

Admittedly, it sounds like an unlikely recipe for success. But taking into account the type of people who open their homes and the type of people who travel across the country pursuing athletic glory, it begins to make sense. A spirit of community makes the host family program work because the families recognize what an event does for the fabric of their community, and they do their part to help it. And events that provide housing for out-of-town racers raise cycling's image within their community by integrating the families into the bike race. For example, it all but guarantees a larger crowd because the host families are invested in seeing their guests compete. Some of cycling's highest-profile races attribute much of their success to the hospitality of their host families.

Every neighborhood in the vicinity of the Redlands Classic becomes an ad hoc hotel for wayward bike racers, and team cars and vans litter the neighborhood streets during race week. More than 100 homeowners sign up as hosts, the majority repeat customers who host the same team year after year.

The Jelly Belly team has returned to the same home for more than 15 years. They know, without having to be told, that you have to jiggle the handle on the bathroom door to get it to latch or that the larger remote controls the volume while the smaller remote changes the channel. They know when the line at Crepes of Wrath is at its shortest and when to avoid it altogether.

Redlands residents Jeff and Raelene Fulford placed their names on the list in 2014. An avid cyclist, Jeff had raced in the amateur ranks at the Redlands Classic, so the idea of hosting pro cyclists didn't seem far-fetched. Raelene was also swept up in the excitement of the event, having been known to rally a friend to stand alongside the course in costume, ringing cowbells and carrying signs. The Fulfords were given the Astellas assignment.

In advance of the team's initial visit, Jeff made room in the garage, and Raelene filled the pantry and hid all the good silverware.

During the team's first year, the Fulfords' experience was typical of a host family. They were excited to have their routine turned upside down, fascinated with the riders, shocked and awed by how much cyclists eat and how much they lie around the house, and dismayed to find that they never had enough toilet paper on hand.

Subsequent years were much easier. When race week arrived, Jeff and Raelene were eager to catch up with "their team," and inevitably disappointed to learn that some riders had left the sport or had been cut loose. Every year, they purchased one more air mattress to make room for yet another rider. The pantry was fuller, the water heater had been upgraded, and there was a stockpile of toilet paper.

For 51 weeks out of the year, Jeff's garage looks like any other cyclist's garage, with a handful of bikes hanging from hooks and a clean and organized space with a Park Tool work stand ready for action at a moment's notice. When Astellas rolled into town, his garage was stuffed to the rafters with 10 road bikes, eight time trial bikes, a stack of spare tires and a larger stack of spare wheels, an air compressor, a garden hose, trainer stands, shipping boxes, shoeboxes, time trial helmets, and boxes of hydration mix and sport gels. And Jeff, a self-proclaimed bike nerd, was in heaven. Amid the chaos, he had the chance to learn tips from pro racers and a pro mechanic. When the team rolled out of town, all his bikes were in tiptop shape.

Of course, host families have their own expertise to offer. Jeff's physical therapy experience was helpful to riders with nagging injuries. Brecht received good advice on dealing with his broken collarbone. When a rider complained of tooth pain, Raelene, a pediatric dentist, was happy to throw on her surgical loupes and inspect the troublesome molar.

Although there was plenty of food in the pantry, the riders were usually on their own for meals because each one had his own caloric schedule to maintain. Consequently, the kitchen was constantly in use. The Fulfords were very accommodating, but they insisted on a family meal on Saturday night, an epic event in which every dish, bowl, fork, knife, and spoon was used. Afterward the riders would insist on helping to clean up, breaking at least one glass in the process. It became as much a tradition as the dinner itself.

Accidents are par for the course. The Fulfords' neighbors were hosting a popular pro team in 2015. When the van arrived loaded with

orange bikes on the roof, it pulled into the driveway, snagged an over-
head cable, and ripped the cable TV feed off the side of the house.
Unfortunately, it happened on the first day of the visit. The Astellas
team chose not to invite them over to the Fulfords' to watch TV. Community has its limits.

Because bike racers stay with host families, they know dogs in
every corner of the country. The Astellas team befriended a border col-
lie named Katy in Silver City, New Mexico, a German shepherd named
Kennedy in Bucks County, Pennsylvania, a malamute in Yucaipa, California, and in Redlands, Jeff and Raelene's labradoodle, Montana.

While the team was walking around in downtown Redlands with
the Fulfords and Montana, a young woman excitedly approached them
to say hello. The riders felt a rush of excitement at being recognized as
celebrities, but she was really saying hello to Montana, who has more
followers on Instagram than the team.

Because canine memory is tied directly to a superior sense of smell,
the dogs remember each rider. When the team returns year after year,
being remembered by a canine friend feels like a true welcome. This
doesn't happen at hotels.

In return for the comforts a host family provides, riders bring a sense
of adventure to the lives of complete strangers. Not all professional
cyclists have an education beyond high school, and even those who do
have clearly chosen a different path, which typically prompts the hosts
to ask about the riders' decision to pursue their dreams. The notion is
mind-boggling to some hosts and as normal as pumpkin pie to others.

"How do your parents feel about you taking time off to race your
bike?" the hosts will ask, often with their own son or daughter within
earshot. The question implies that there is something else more important that is being neglected, but the Astellas riders who strung together
a few seasons learned to handle this deftly.

Aitcheson, Murfet, Feehery, and Green each developed a mono-
logue to explain their lifestyle. Just as a movie star repeats the same

pat answers on a junket, the riders carefully edited and revised their spiel to avoid any tone of superiority. The dinner table conversations revealed that many people harbor envy, regret, and occasionally unbridled resentment at not having pursued their own dreams. Pressure to join the working world may have stymied a dream of backpacking across Europe or studying music. If the riders didn't play the situation just right, they could be caught in a tug of war between parents and their children. So they diplomatically chose to ride the middle road.

In most cases, host families were rooting for their guests to continue living the dream, which prompted the riders to regale the host family with stories of life on the road until late into the night.

At the Bucks County event in Pennsylvania, Astellas stayed with some empty-nesters who had begrudgingly allowed their neighbors to talk them into playing host for the first time. On the first day, the couple shied away from direct interaction. On the second day, they ventured into the basement, where the team was housed to ask a few questions. Their demeanors softened when they heard the riders' individual stories. By Saturday, they had a newfound fascination for cycling, and the entire group enjoyed meaningful conversation during a cookout in the backyard. When it came time to say goodbye on Sunday, the hosts had become the type that would convince their doubting neighbors to take in a team, thus extending the circle.

The Bucks County race was a team favorite that year despite its miserably windy, rainy, and cold race conditions due in large part to the community's support and homegrown hospitality.

In contrast, there are times when a team never even see their hosts. At the Tour of America's Dairyland in 2014, Astellas arrived to find an envelope containing the house keys and a note that read: "Help yourself to whatever you need! Have a great week!" By the end of the week, they had felt as though they had stayed in a very comfortable hotel, which meant they missed out on the thrill of converting an unbeliever into a cycling fan or, at the very least, mixing with the locals.

Because the sport can offer so many lonely moments, the Astellas riders preferred the sense of community afforded by the host family housing plan. It made life on the road more enjoyable and created lasting friendships. Still today, they receive a pile of Christmas cards and they can recommend a great dentist in Redlands.

CHAPTER 14

FINDING THE RIGHT FORMULA

Near the very end of 2014, Frey received a call from a popular pro on a WorldTour team who recommended that Frey take on a particular rider for the coming season. Frey knew this rider was in his late thirties and he already had a mentor in mind for the team, so he declined the offer. Intent on using his influence to find a team for this rider, the caller pushed Frey harder. Frey declined again. Insults ensued, but in the end Frey stuck to his original plan.

Team directors are regularly approached by well-intentioned individuals campaigning on behalf of the next Greg LeMerckx. If there is a preexisting connection between the team and the ad hoc agent, or if the agent has the credentials to back up the recommendation, it has a good chance of working. In fact, teams rely on it. When Frankie Andreu spoke up, Frey listened. Joe Holmes, David Wenger, and others had the advantage of a professional connection with Frey. Attempts to strong-arm management decisions do happen, but Frey firmly believed that conceding to cold calls from casual acquaintances, however prominent, didn't serve the team's best interests.

Four years into being a team manager, Frey had developed an eye for talent and more leverage. If he could make the deal that he had in mind, the mentor he intended to sign would bring tremendous racing experience to Astellas.

At 43 years of age, Adam Myerson was looking to race one last season at the pro level before retiring. He had spent five years riding for the Mountain Khakis team, which morphed into the SmartStop team. Frey had been talking with Myerson about riding for a young developmental team for about 10 years, but he wasn't in a position to make it a reality until 2015.

Frey and Curin never had any qualms about Myerson's age. It was clear that he could still go fast and suffer willingly—two of the most basic requirements for bike racing. They respected Myerson's strong anti-doping stance and appreciated that he didn't allow himself to become jaded by the sport.

Bike racing sees its fair share of burnout. Endless travel and hard racing while getting paid a pittance can wear a rider down. It's common for cyclists to feel unappreciated or cheated out of a chance to succeed. Riders entering the sport with illusions of making it to the Tour de France often become embittered when others climb the ladder with comparative ease. It's not easy to succeed in cycling, and the sheer amount of work required to be mediocre can cause the sport to seem unfair.

Myerson endured all of it. He still loved to race his bike after 25 years in the saddle. An outspoken opponent of doping, he had a personality strong enough to either galvanize a team or drive them crazy, depending on their outlook. He was a welcome addition to Astellas, and the younger riders were eager to learn from him.

Among them was Dan Gardner, a 19-year-old from Brighton, England, who showed great mettle at races in England at the end of the 2014 season, earning Green's recommendation. A typically polite Brit with great cycling instincts, Gardner was the youngest rider the team had ever signed. His salary was paid by the Dave Rayner Fund, a British-based nonprofit organization that provides grants to promising young cyclists.

His trip from the pastoral countryside of southern England to the United States was his initiation into the American experience. His flight from New York to Milwaukee was canceled, forcing him to find accommodations in New York City. The cheapest room available nearly emptied his wallet. At 3 a.m. a violent fight broke out in the room next door. He waited for the sound of gunfire until jet lag caused him to drift off to sleep again. When morning finally came, he nearly missed his flight. By the time he arrived in Milwaukee, Gardner was earnestly questioning his decision to race in the States. He reached out to the Dave Rayner Fund to report the misadventure and look for a way out of it, but they wasted no time in convincing him to stay put.

Jake Silverberg had dominated the cycling scene in Miami, Florida, for a year or so and was ready for new horizons. Just 20 years old, he had won the junior national championship road race a year before, but hadn't yet found a team for the 2015 season. His coach had been watching his power numbers and felt that Silverberg had what it took to compete at a higher level. He reached out to a friend connected with Astellas and asked him to take a look at Silverberg's résumé. Based on the recommendation that followed, Silverberg's results, and a phone interview, Frey offered him a spot.

Jake Sitler came to the team from the Van Dessel amateur squad. He was a steeplechaser at Shippensburg University in Pennsylvania before turning to cycling. He had track and field to thank for his lung capacity, but a competitive fire was his true advantage. As the story goes, he was at the campus natatorium with his cross-country teammates when they decided to have a contest to see who could stay underwater the longest. An incoming freshman proceeded to swim two full lengths of the pool without taking a breath, and Sitler couldn't let him go unchallenged. He swam two full lengths and made a turn to begin the third length. A few strokes into the third lap, he sank to the bottom of the pool. He was so determined to win that he almost drowned. His teammates had to fish him out and resuscitate him.

On the bike, Sitler won the King of the Mountains (KOM) jersey at the Bucks County Classic, got on the podium in an NCC race, and lapped the field at his first criterium national championships. He was a racehorse with raw talent.

Max Jenkins and Peter Olejniczak came to the team from opposite ends of the experience spectrum. At age 28, Max had logged more miles on the international racing scene than any rider in Astellas's short history. He rode on the United Healthcare team at the Pro Continental level and with Competitive Cyclist and 5-Hour Energy teams at the Conti level. He was part of the USAC National Team program after winning the 2007 U23 National Championships, racing in Europe and Asia multiple times. He also had significant stage-race experience at Amgen, Utah, and Alberta.

Peter, on the other hand, just 22 years old, was a former professional cross-country skier with two bike-race wins to his name: an NCC race and a stage of Intelligentsia Cup. Despite their busy race schedules, both Jenkins and Olejniczak found time to get a college education. Jenkins had a degree in economics from the University of California at Berkeley, and Olejniczak had graduated summa cum laude from the University of North Dakota with a degree in aerospace science and air traffic control at the age of 20.

Slackers.

WHILE THE BUDGET DIDN'T necessarily show a surplus, Curin and Frey felt it was necessary to hold a training camp prior to the first race of the 2015 season. Their previous attempt had delivered only limited results, but it seemed worthwhile to try again.

An Astellas oncologist had invited the team to a ride in Tampa and there was also a full race weekend scheduled, including an NRC race. It seemed an excellent opportunity for the team to kick off their season, so Curin opted to kill three birds with one stone and hold the team camp in nearby Polk City, Florida.

Opportunity comes with hard knocks, and Polk City and the surrounding area were not ideal for riding. Motorists in the Orlando vicinity regularly drive as if they're outrunning a hurricane, and the terrain is as flat as a garage floor. But Curin had been begging for another opportunity to interface with Astellas customers for the past two years. Anything he could do to provide value to Astellas would bolster his team's status at the home office.

The team rented a six-bedroom house and as everyone started to arrive, it felt like a family reunion. A positive vibe remained from the prior season, and the returning riders were happy to welcome their new teammates.

The garage and driveway looked like a bomb had gone off in a bike shop with wheels, bikes, boxes, clothing, and bike parts scattered everywhere. Kelley was working frantically to assemble bikes that had arrived just days before, not in December when he had all the time in the world.

The subdivision consisted of rental properties filled with vacationers who drove by in wide-eyed wonder as they saw 16 riders fidgeting with their bikes and trying on clothes.

Each evening Frey briefed the team on their sponsorship responsibilities and what to say about Astellas and the equipment suppliers in post-race interviews though it was unlikely that anyone would ask them anything about Astellas that required more than a few words.

There wasn't much to say about the supporting cast of sponsors. Pactimo was back as their clothing supplier. Justin Williams had designed a new kit modeled after European soccer jerseys. Solid red, it was a real departure from the black jerseys crowding the peloton. There would be no hiding in the pack this year.

Williams had also made a connection with FFWD Wheels, which provided clincher trainers and very fast tubular rims. Ritchey gave them a box of components that were every bit as good as any other manufacturer's. Limar provided helmets that were everything a helmet should be. Bollé sent sunglasses and T-shirts. Soigneur supplied chamois butter and embrocation for cold-weather riding. They were committed to speaking positively about every brand that contributed to outfitting the team.

They were urged to mention their suppliers on social media, even though the general public seemed numb to the dreck (hashtags, likes, mentions, shares, etc.) that cluttered timelines. The riders knew their sponsors followed along, hoping to see their brands pop up with regularity, though few ever gave any feedback to the team. Their posts seemingly disappeared into a black hole.

Things seemed to be looking up for the team, but the best was yet to come. Pro riders live for the moment when new bikes are delivered. The thrill of assembling a new bike with new components never gets old.

Curin had negotiated the bike deal with Litespeed prior to the 2014 season. According to the contract he drafted, Litespeed would provide the team with a given number of frames for three years. The company's accountants interpreted the wording literally, so Litespeed would indeed provide frames for three years, but they wouldn't be providing new frames each year. When the boxes containing 2014-model framesets arrived, the team couldn't help but feel slighted. It was like receiving a hand-me-down sweater.

The loophole was a bitter pill to swallow for Curin, who was still learning the ins and outs of team management. Also per the contract, Litespeed only sent enough frames to replace the broken ones from the previous season.

THEY LOOKED LIKE a professional outfit as they rolled a double paceline down the Florida road, but the magic of the formation was lost on the motorists, buzzing by at 60 mph just inches away from the riders. The team's training rides in the Polk City area consisted of a nervous 15 miles on a busy two-lane road. Once they got to the paved Van Fleet Trail, the team could ride indefinitely without having to deal with motorists. It was a mind-numbingly straight and flat stretch, only marginally better than riding an indoor trainer. However, they did see an alligator, which never happens on an indoor trainer.

Off the bike, the better part of one day was spent aimlessly driving around in search of a decent backdrop for the team photo. Central Florida is a popular tourist destination thanks to the theme parks, but team photos typically feature an impressive landscape, not a swamp. They settled on an industrial backdrop. Individual photos were shot from the car while the riders dodged trucks hauling oranges and tourists rushing to and from the Disney complexes.

For the experienced riders photo day was part of the job; for the younger riders the attention felt uncomfortable. But everyone agreed that the greater Orlando area was not the place to do it.

THE SATURDAY MORNING RIDE with the Astellas customer required the team to be up and out by 5:30 a.m. They misjudged the drive time and arrived precisely when the ride was scheduled to begin, at 7.00 a.m. Jumping out of the team van, they hurriedly readied their bikes and noticed that the group was already starting to roll out. The team took off on their bikes as the group headed onto the Gandy Boulevard Bridge. It was as if the ride had been launched from a trebuchet. Their noses were pressed firmly on their stems as they rode 35 mph to catch up amid Tampa's morning rush hour traffic.

Coming off the Gandy Bridge into St. Petersburg, the pack made a left-hand turn across three lanes of traffic in front of oncoming cars like bank robbers escaping a heist. Then another abrupt left-hand turn heading the wrong way on a merge ramp. Ten minutes into a two-hour ride, the team had cheated death three times. The hair-raising events continued for the duration of the ride.

When pro riders attend a local group ride, they are typically unaware of the local rules, customs, and routes. They are at the mercy of the group.

Whether it stems from a disappointment in not having reached the pro level, a feeling that pro riders are excessively pampered, or a simple need to prove themselves, there is a contingent that thrives on making life difficult for any pro rider who shows up for a local ride. On a ride such as the one in St. Petersburg, local heroes will leverage an out-of-towner's unfamiliarity to get the upper hand. There's no warning about a hazardous corner that always gathers loose sand, or they purposely remain quiet about a steep hill around the next bend, figuring a big-time pro bike racer will be able to handle it.

Indeed, they can handle it. Still, a pro rider knows to keep his or her head on a swivel to spot the hidden traps. They also place a lot of faith in the fact that however badly these riders want glory, they don't want to get killed.

Throughout the ride, the Astellas riders tried to figure out which of the locals in the pack was the doctor who had invited them. After three hours of riding in St. Petersburg, the group returned and dispersed without a word. The team found out later that the doctor never showed up. It is possible that they had joined the wrong ride altogether. There's no way of knowing. And no one on the team heard from the doctor again.

Frey was dumbfounded at having spent close to $15,000 in airfare, housing, food, and gas to hold a training camp in Florida to appease one oncologist who never bothered to notify them that he wouldn't be attending. In the future Frey resolved to spell out the requirements of activation rides in great detail. As it turned out, this would be the only such ride for the season.

JUST DAYS BEFORE TRAINING CAMP began, the team learned that two of the races had been canceled. The Gasparilla Criterium and time trial, which were on USAC's NCC calendar, had been expected to draw all the big teams, including United Healthcare. When the race was canceled, the other teams stayed away, leaving Astellas as the only pro team to race the Pinellas Park Circuit Race on Sunday.

Astellas would eventually split into a road team and crit team for the season, but everyone kitted up for this race. They were confident about their chances. With 16 riders, they made up one-quarter of the 64-rider field.

The first breakaway to form contained 10 riders, including two Astellas riders. Mathematically, this move diminished their odds of winning by 5 percent.

It's a mistake that amateur teams frequently make, ending up with a smaller percentage of riders in the breakaway than they have in the race itself. Usually, amateur teams are just happy to have a teammate in the breakaway, so they care less about odds and instead focus on working to make the breakaway succeed. Adam Myerson and Clay Murfet knew better. They helped to reel in the breakaway in order to shuffle the cards and try again with better numbers.

The next breakaway to gain any sort of gap contained six riders, including three from Astellas. This time, the field collectively disagreed with the mix and worked to bring it back.

The race continued with various combinations establishing a lead only to be sucked in. At some point, it became apparent that there were just two teams in the race: Astellas and everyone else.

When a three-man breakaway formed off the front containing no Astellas riders, the other teams worked to disrupt the chase and prevent Astellas from joining the leaders. Astellas worked hard to bring the breakaway back, but they were unable to control the last lap, and they lost the race to Team Cocos's Yosmani Rodriguez. Monk finished second. Hogan Sills was seventh.

It was a disappointing and somewhat embarrassing first outing for the team. They were, by far, the strongest team in the race, both in terms of experience and sheer numbers, yet they lacked cohesion.

On that sour note at Pinellas Park, camp ended, and the team packed up and split up to conquer the season.

CHAPTER 15

SEASON 4: THE RED ARMY MARCHES ON

The logistics of a cycling team can be tricky, and any number of things can foul the works.

In late March, Silverberg, Gardner, and Sitler landed at LAX for the San Dimas Stage Race and found themselves stranded without a ride. The team van had been waylaid by a mechanical issue in Texas and wouldn't arrive until the next day. They called Frey in Milwaukee, who discovered that a cheap hotel near LAX would cost about $20 less than a 50-mile Uber ride to San Dimas, so he booked a room for the three cyclists. The cab driver gave the squeaky-clean athletes a sideways look as he dropped them off at their hotel, as if to say, "Are we sure we have the right place?"

Staying in sketchy hotels is part of a Continental cyclist's life, and this one was typically sketchy. As they entered the room they noticed what looked like a bullet hole near the door. The room was filthy, and once the guys saw the condition of the bathroom and towels they decided that they didn't need to shower. They slept in their clothes and on top of the bedding because they were wary of bedbugs, and Sitler kept a saddle and seat post next to his pillow for protection. For what it's worth, 3T makes a very stout and confidence-inspiring seat post. At

6 a.m., someone tried entering their room, but the dead bolt prevailed. By 7 a.m., the entire hotel reeked of marijuana, and by 7:30 a.m., the trio called an Uber driver, who loaded their gear into his car and took them to a nearby beach where they waited for the team van to arrive.

Several hours later, they made it to their host family's home in San Dimas, where they met up with the rest of the team. They could finally relax and focus on the race.

From the start, the race didn't go smoothly. Sitler was hyper-focused on his warm-up for the time trial and missed his start time by 10 seconds. In the first few miles he overcompensated and went anaerobic but recovered quickly and managed a top-20 finish.

In stage 2, Silverberg crashed early, while Sitler got tangled up in the chaotic feed zone and was taken down. His bike couldn't be fixed by banging on it with his fists, and he lost time waiting for help from a mechanic.

Feed zone crashes aren't unusual. There are no training manuals for soigneurs who work in the feed zone—just an implied code and an obscure set of unwritten rules—and as a result, feed zones are the most dangerous stretch of a road race course. The professional soigneurs, who tend to give amateur feed zone workers a wide berth, can hand bottles from a standing position without flinching, while the amateur soigneurs usually run alongside their rider and still drop their bottle.

In this case, it was an amateur team with a well-intentioned family member acting as soigneur that caused the tangle. Unfortunately, Sitler had been Astellas's highest-placed rider and overall contender, so the team spent the rest of the weekend chasing individual placings.

Late in the crash-marred second stage, Max and Cortlan's desperate jailbreak was reeled in with a kilometer to go and the two placed outside the top 20. Some riders posted encouraging results. Green sprinted to ninth place in the second stage, while Brecht cracked the top 15 in Sunday's criterium. For Gardner, San Dimas was his first look at American racing. He didn't have much to work with, but he had plenty to write home about.

On the Monday after the race, the guys met up with some Astellas employees for an easy ride on the road race loop. Conversation hobbled along as the two groups had little in common aside from the logo printed on the jerseys, but the Astellas group was excited to ride with professional cyclists, and they made all the standard jokes about attaching bungie cords to their handlebars. For the Astellas riders, it was fun to give pointers and show off a bit, and they were eager to solidify the connection between the team and the Astellas mothership.

Brecht skipped the corporate ride and headed straight to the Fulfords' house in Redlands to enjoy some last-minute training rides prior to the Redlands Classic the following weekend. He loved riding in Southern California and used the Fulfords' home as a base camp.

Riding along the coast is a novelty for most foreign riders. The sun was shining on Southern California, and the water and sand were gorgeous. Brecht thought it was the perfect setting for a selfie. While attempting to take the photo, he fell and snapped his collarbone.

The news that Brecht was out for Redlands quickly spread to his teammates. He was embarrassed, and the team was disappointed. He had been their best hope for a top finish on the General Classification at Redlands and other races in April and May. (Brecht was dejected but determined to bounce back quickly. While most doctors advise that a broken collarbone needs six weeks to heal, he was back on the bike and racing in three weeks' time.)

Against stiff competition at Redlands, the team struggled with results. Not having a true G.C. contender meant that they would try to focus on individual stage wins, but that didn't pan out. In stage 1, Jenkins was the highest-placed Astellas rider in 34th. Cortlan took enough points to win the KOM jersey but would relinquish it a few days later when his competition gobbled up points via a breakaway. The best the team could get at the Big Bear time trial was 86th place. Sitler wrapped it up with 16th in the mountaintop finish on the Oak Glen stage. On the way back down the mountain, the team wasn't speaking much—the air in the team van was heavy with fatigue and defeat.

The final day's criterium wasn't a great outing for the road squad, either, although Sitler managed to grab 13th place. For a guy who preferred road races, he demonstrated some serious pack skills in the criterium but still made it known that he had no interest in jumping to the crit squad.

Despite the lack of results, the team was enjoying their weekend in Redlands. Their evenings were spent around the backyard campfire playing games and sharing their stories with the Fulfords. They had a great host family who made their stay almost too comfortable.

FIVE WEEKS LATER, members of the crit squad went to California to race the Dana Point Grand Prix. In previous years Williams had raced well there, and he felt confident that his form was the best it had been all season. In April, he circled May 5 on his calendar and asked Frey to send a full squad. United Healthcare and the Hincapie Racing Team would be there for the NCC points offered to top finishers, and Williams felt it would be his best opportunity to beat the UHC Blue Train, and anyone else who showed up.

Aitcheson was also coming into good form with fifth-place finishes at the Roswell Criterium and the Athens Twilight in Georgia. He took third at the Novant Health Invitational in Charlotte, North Carolina, and rode well at Speed Week in South Carolina. Although he hadn't won a race yet this season, he had established his ability to get into a lot of breakaways, so Frey made a last-minute decision to send him out west to Dana Point.

With both Aitcheson and Williams racing well, it created the classic dilemma: Who would the team work for?

The Dana Point Grand Prix is a fast L-shaped criterium with wide turns that allow the field to go full gas without much worry and just a few small undulations to help break things up. A breakaway of four established a lead of 25 seconds midway through the race. Aitcheson went on the attack with Ty Magner (Hincapie), David Santos (KHS-Maxxis-JLVelo), and Karl Menzies (United Healthcare). They were joined by two more riders late in the race.

Back in the field, the loyalties of the Astellas team were split. Some riders on the squad felt that Aitcheson would place third at best, behind Magner and Menzies. They wanted to bring the breakaway back and let Williams try to win in a field sprint. Others, including crit squad captain Myerson, wanted the breakaway to succeed so Aitcheson could go for the win.

It's a conflict that almost every team faces at some point. Riders instinctively know when they're on great form and Williams knew how to win on the Dana Point course, but when a teammate gets into position to win the race, a choice needs to be made. The team had to choose between Aitcheson, who had ridden consistently but hadn't won yet, and Williams, who had won some races but wasn't in the best position to win this race.

After a fair amount of bickering, the team put their support behind Aitcheson, who stayed away with the break and held on for third place. Williams ended up crashing on the last lap. In his mind, the team squandered an opportunity.

It took Williams several weeks to get over the sting of Dana Point. He believed he had the legs to win, and he had specifically targeted that race and requested support. The crash only made it worse.

He would be back, but not immediately.

THE CRIT SQUAD WAS LOOKING forward to making the trip to Wisconsin in late June for the Tour of America's Dairyland, or TOAD. With 11 races in 11 days, there were plenty of opportunities to win cash, and this year Astellas felt they had the riders to do it. The crit squad was motivated, and Williams was back from his cooling-off period and ready to race.

One of the more popular stages takes place at Schlitz Park in Milwaukee, the site of the original Schlitz Beer complex, which has been redeveloped into a vibrant community. The Schlitz Park course is eight-tenths of a mile in length, with a long straight uphill between turns one and two and a long, snaking descent between turns three through eight. It is one of the hardest courses in the sport because it requires a combination of great climbing strength and superior descending skills. The downhill section winds through a neighborhood of stately homes on tree-lined streets. There is only one good line on the descent, and it's exactly six inches wide. If a rider deviates from that line, he will either scrub off speed and lose ground, or lose control and crash. Recessed manholes, crowned roads, off-camber turns, and odd turn angles demand an arsenal of bike-handling skills. And it's crazy fast. When gaps begin to form in the peloton, riders immediately become vocal because there aren't too many places on the course where time can be made up. To close a gap on the flat homestretch spends precious energy that will be needed on the climb. Any gap between riders usually spells the beginning of the end for riders on the wrong side of it.

Early in the race, Myerson found himself in a breakaway with Australian legend Jack Bobridge (Budget Forklifts) and about six other riders. A six-time world champion in the individual and team pursuit, a seven-time Australian national champion, and a two-time Olympic silver medalist, Bobridge also had four Giros d'Italia on his race résumé. A Bobridge-led breakaway was almost a guaranteed success.

By his own admission, Myerson is not the best climber, and as the race progressed, he found himself struggling. But he's one of the best bike handlers, with superior cornering skills, so instead of killing himself to stay with the breakaway on the climb, he paced himself and allowed a small gap to open up between himself and the breakaway every time they went up. On the downhill he used his descending and cornering skills to quickly close the gap again. In essence, he was riding in his own solo breakaway very near, but only briefly, with Bobridge's breakaway. Each time they passed the finish line, the crowd saw seven riders riding together in a breakaway group. Elsewhere on the course, it was a group of six with Myerson in pursuit.

This was the type of strategy that a seasoned racer like Myerson shared with his younger Astellas teammates. Where a younger rider would panic if a gap opened up between them and the breakaway, Myerson knew how to work it.

Had the other riders in the breakaway taken note of what Myerson was doing, they might have conserved enough energy on the Schlitz Park climb to remain in the lead group. But the race was winding down, and now just three riders survived, having managed to lap the field: Myerson, Bobridge, and Benjamin Hill. Unfortunately, Myerson had nothing left on that final trip up the hill and resigned himself to a third-place finish.

Myerson also taught the younger riders that it's sometimes necessary, and perfectly okay, to talk to the other riders in the breakaway. Early in the Schlitz Park breakaway, Myerson realized that he wasn't going to be able to take his share of pulls at the speed they were going. He told the group that he would contribute now and then, but their 100 percent effort was faster than his. They let him stay in the breakaway, which allowed him to end up on the podium, when a more aggressive strategy would have been to shed him.

Two days later on a flat course at Neenah, the team agreed that it was going to be Stephen Hyde's day. Myerson was patrolling the front early in the race when Bobridge made a move off the front with Omar Mendoza of Ciclismo Meta Colombia and Grant Erhard, riding for SBR Quantum Racing. Myerson tagged along with them so that Hyde could sit in the pack and conserve energy.

As usual, Bobridge was flying. He drove the breakaway hard, and they quickly built a lead that was never to be challenged. When Myerson's breakaway group lapped the field, his Astellas teammates met him at the rear of the peloton and dragged him straight to the front in case another attack went off containing Bobridge or the other break-away companions.

With ten laps to go, the Red Army of Astellas drove the pace in order to discourage any late attacks. In this situation, a selfish rider might focus on attaining the highest place possible for himself. Knowing that Myerson had guaranteed a top-five finish by lapping the field with four others, a teammate could attempt to win the field sprint for sixth place. But when the team has a chance to take first, no matter how remote that chance is, an unselfish rider doesn't consider sprinting.

Williams, who felt that Myerson had prevented him from winning at Dana Point, was in a good position to contest the sprint. He knew he could win it, but with an Astellas rider in position to win the race, nothing else mattered. The seven-week cooling-off period had done its job.

Williams and Monk were the last two members of the lead-out train, with Myerson sitting in the catbird seat in third place. They were driving the pace hard in order to keep him in position, and it was Williams's job to get them through the penultimate corner. Once he had done that, his day would be finished and Monk would take over and deliver Myerson to the line.

Down the backstretch, however, Bobridge's team tried to go over the top of Astellas, or pass the Astellas lead-out train. There's nothing untoward about the move. It's a race, after all, and whoever can go faster is free to go. Williams looked over at the Budget Forklifts team and quickly accelerated to the corner, taking Monk and Myerson with him. Just as they hit the turn, Monk hit a pothole that caused his chain to jump off his front chainring. He lost all his momentum and pulled out of the line. Myerson yelled and Williams dug a little deeper. Instead of dropping off as planned, he stayed on the front doing the work of two men, pulling Myerson to the final turn at a speed no one could challenge.

As they rounded the final turn, Williams peeled off. Myerson sprinted and was passed by a handful of riders. He quickly looked around to see if Bobridge, Mendoza, or Erhard had passed him. They hadn't, so Myerson, by virtue of having lapped the field, won the race.

It was just one win in a long series of races, but the team's two best sprinters rode for Myerson, demonstrating their maturity.

The next day in Waukesha, Monk found his way into a breakaway with 10 other riders and lapped the field. With the help of his teammates, he fought his way to the front of the field and won the sprint to take the win. He had come a long way from the days of the Astellas Oncology team, when he was doing well to finish third in a regional race. Now he was reading the races correctly, getting into the right moves, and finishing with wins.

THE RED ARMY'S CRITERIUM TEAM was learning that bike racing requires much more than simply going fast. There were tactics and lessons, and the easygoing Myerson had a gift for teaching them. Having had a coaching business of his own, his methods were honed to a few basic principles: talk plainly, don't lecture, be empathetic and not pedantic.

Myerson encouraged his teammates to ride by feel instead of fixating on their power meters. He wanted them to treat the race as a bike race, not a math problem. Amateur riders frequently focus on their wattage during a race, unlike most pro riders. Many pro riders go so far as to put electrical tape over the heart rate and wattage data fields. Green had a reputation for blazing criteriums with a single piece of information displayed on his device: running time.

On the road squad, Jenkins was the mentor and he had as much or more experience as Myerson to share. It was a slower teaching process in road races when days and weeks would pass between events. Contrasted with TOAD, which had 11 classroom sessions in as many days, the road calendar had only a few weekends with multiple road races. And once a rider gets dropped from the main field in a road race, the rest of the day is spent riding in a small group to the finish line, at which point there aren't a lot of tactics to learn. If they could hold on, younger riders could tap Jenkins's vast knowledge of each race and the courses they were held on. Over the course of his bike racing career, he had competed at Redlands multiple times and had finished in the top 10 at Gila. He usually knew how race action would play out.

ASTELLAS ASKED THAT the team attend the 12th annual Ride for Roswell, a charity ride in Buffalo, New York, in June. More than 7,200 amateur riders took part, and the local Astellas sales reps were out in force, helping to raise more than $4 million for the Roswell Park Comprehensive Cancer Institute. The appearance of the pro cycling team created excitement in the Astellas tent, where reps and families mingled with the riders and had photos taken.

Continental riders usually feel uneasy about being treated like stars. They know that they're at the bottom of the bike racing ladder, so the attention can feel unwarranted or undeserved. But the people who attend such events are inspired by the chance to interact with athletes wearing a pro kit. Eventually, the Astellas riders succumbed to the adoration and had a great time.

In the days that followed, one of the sales reps wrote a glowing letter of praise to the home office, declaring it a brilliant idea to have a professional cycling team representing them at charity rides such as Ride for Roswell. The letter was shared with the team and everyone agreed that this was precisely the sort of feel-good inroad necessary to win the hearts of the global headquarters.

LATER IN THE 2015 SEASON, Curin had his eye on the horizon, ever on the lookout for potential replacements should Astellas choose to end their agreement. His long-term goal was to advance the team to the next level of competition, but he was well aware that finding a sponsor to simply maintain what he already had would be challenging enough. Out of the blue, he received a phone call from a marketing consultant offering to conduct a free sponsorship search for the team. Kevin York, a cycling and triathlon fan, had recently started his own company and was anxious to grow his client list. He was a godsend for Curin. Having someone else looking for out-of-industry sponsors took away one of the more onerous tasks of team management. With his own role limited to nights and weekends, he welcomed any effort to find more money, and because York was working solely on commission, it wasn't going to cost the team anything up front.

York immediately got to work contacting companies of all sizes. He pursued every promising lead, and quickly became frustrated by the preponderance of roadblocks. Often his first connection with a company was with lower-ranking personnel who understood cycling, but by the time their proposal reached the desk of the company's chief trigger-puller, it would die a quick death. He discovered that most people in influential positions just didn't "get" cycling.

All the usual arguments against advertising in the sport came up when York spoke with companies like Allstate, Takata, and UBS: There's no revenue, a limited audience, no TV, no activation; bike racing is difficult to understand. These were all things that Curin knew. In a nutshell, there was simply no return on investment.

Two large companies that supported pro baseball and football said they didn't want to touch cycling as a result of the Lance Armstrong drug scandal. But the negative responses mostly came down to the negligible number of impressions to be had—not enough people would see their product.

From a business standpoint, a company with $300,000 to spend on sports marketing can purchase space on the boards surrounding the ice at a National Hockey League arena that will be seen by roughly 18,000 spectators at 40 home games, in addition to a TV audience that numbers in the thousands. The sponsoring company also receives the right to use the NHL team's logo on marketing materials, declaring it an official team sponsor. And the company gets an arena expo booth that gives them access to thousands of walk-up customers each night.

That same $300,000 would have funded the Astellas team for the entire season, but how many people would see the company's logo?

In the fall of 2015, York traveled to New York City for a meeting with a large bank with close to a trillion dollars in assets. He knew that they were heavily involved with sponsorship in two other sports and that it would be tough to get them to add a third, but he went to the meeting with a killer presentation and impressed the first wave of decision-makers. His hopes skyrocketed; he took a deep breath and pressed on. Somewhere in the third or fourth wave of his pitch, things fell apart. Someone with the authority to kill the idea killed it. They knew nothing about cycling and saw no value in learning, and York went home empty-handed.

Once back in Chicago, he met with some heavy hitters who had worked with the Chicago Cubs and other major sports properties. He didn't make it halfway through his presentation before the top dog shook his head and said, "Not worth the time." The group made its exit before York could collect his things. Cycling was a far cry from being the instant plug-and-play moneymaker they were after.

After many months of trying, York managed to get a couple of token sponsorships, such as in-kind product offerings on par with the free socks that are handed out at Interbike. But otherwise he rode the same roller coaster enjoyed by a thousand sponsor seekers before him: His hopes shot up whenever he received a morsel of encouragement, only to plummet a few weeks later.

He made headway with another large pharmaceutical company, but they weren't motivated to move as fast as the Astellas team needed them to. Business relationships take time to foster, and advertising budgets take shape more than a year in advance. Even if the new sponsor had been all in, it wouldn't have been ready in time to save the team.

Meanwhile, it was costing York money to chase golden goose eggs. The other side of his business grew into other sports that actually paid him, and he stopped working for Astellas.

By that time, Curin was fully aware that the winds of change were blowing at gale force within Astellas, and it was a matter of time before the cycling budget would catch the attention of someone who had the power to divert it elsewhere.

AS THE SEASON WINDS DOWN each year, a team director's thoughts turn to the following season and questions arise: What were our strengths and weaknesses? Which riders will stay, and which ones are leaving? Who is available? Who can we afford?

It was during this time in 2015 that Frey received a call from another team director who had seen Astellas grow quickly in its first two years as a pro team and wanted to offer a solution to the problem of sponsorship acquisition. He suggested that the two teams merge.

He had obviously given it a lot of thought. His elaborate plan put him in the director's spot at all the races, leaving Frey to manage the logistics from his home in Milwaukee. He had a big bike shop in California lined up and ready to take on a major role. He also had a "bunch of industry sponsors" ready to ship bikes, clothing, food, and equipment. They were just waiting for the green light. And for his services, he would accept a salary of $60,000.

Throughout its existence, no one on the Astellas staff made anything close to $60,000. Not even half that amount.

In addition to offering his services as team director, he insisted that four of his riders join the team for no less than $12,000 each.

Throughout the team's entire existence, very few of the Astellas riders made a $12,000 salary; zero was closer to average.

Frey suppressed laughter as he declined the offer and its $108,000 price tag.

The scenario is somewhat common in cycling. Team directors enjoy a taste of success and believe they're on the path to becoming a WorldTour director, so they become out of touch with racing at the Continental level. The hard truth is that no one makes $60,000 as a team director unless they are also filling water bottles, booking hotel rooms, loading the car, and winning poker tournaments.

Frey considered it to be an odd, backhanded compliment that someone would want to take his team away from him. It meant that it had value, though he wasn't sure what that value was. They certainly looked professional, and he took pride in how his riders handled themselves on and off the bike. They had a good reputation among other racers. If that attracted hostile takeover attempts, he was flattered, but neither he nor Curin was interested.

Having been turned down, the team director vowed to bury Astellas at the upcoming races. It was the last they ever heard from him.

THERE WAS BUZZ BUILDING around the 2015 UCI Road World Championships, which were to be held in Richmond, Virginia, in late September. Normally, this wouldn't affect the Astellas team because historically the worlds were exclusively for national teams. But a 2012 rule change allowed riders to race in the team time trial (TTT) event with their sponsored trade team instead of their country's national team. In addition, because of the UCI rating for the world championships, Continental teams from the host country were eligible to enter the race at their discretion.

This meant that Astellas had an opportunity to race against the top WorldTour teams, something they had never done. They would be on the same course in the same race with the biggest names in cycling, in front of the largest crowds they had ever seen.

The conversation among team members throughout June and July reflected the momentous opportunity as well as the reservations felt by some riders:

"No. We aren't going."

"We are definitely going."

"No way. We'll embarrass ourselves. We'll finish dead last."

"It'll be a great experience."

"It'll be humiliating."

"So? How often are worlds held in our backyard?"

"You guys. Do not go."

"We're going."

The veterans knew what was likely to happen—they would be trounced—but the younger riders didn't care. Mechanic Matt Kelley, who knew what it took to move six riders and six bikes around the country, predicted it would be "an utter logistical nightmare." Frey pondered the decision briefly and concluded that it was a unique experience his riders wouldn't get elsewhere. Sure, it had the potential to be a disaster, but he was willing to take the risk.

If the team was going to go, a lot of details needed to come together quickly. They would need someone to replace Matt Kelley, who was unable to make the trip, so freelance mechanic Gary Bavolar filled in. Each rider would need a time trial bike and an aero helmet, along with pristine team skinsuits (theirs were ripped from prior crashes). Most importantly, they would need to find time to train together while the regular racing season marched on. None of them had ever ridden in a six-man team time trial.

The most difficult order of business was finding six riders who were willing to race. The TTT requires a different level of commitment and a different style of training. It would mean setting aside regular season goals and focusing only on time trialing skills, because no rider, no matter how experienced, can simply show up and ride well. Not racing the regular schedule meant forfeiting any chance at prize money, which is a tough choice for riders who rely on prize money as income. Eventually, Gardner, Feehery, Brown, Jenkins, Sitler, and Silverberg each committed. A pure sprinter, Feehery was ill-suited for the long steady effort of a TTT, but he figured it would be similar to riding in a breakaway. Plus, they needed six guys.

Each of the equipment sponsors stepped up with contributions to the effort. A call was placed to Litespeed asking for time trial bikes.

Because it was late in their production cycle, inventory was low, so they were only able to provide four of the six needed. Two riders would have to ride their personal time trial bikes. Limar went above and beyond the sponsorship agreement and provided six of their best aerodynamic helmets. Pactimo printed up custom, long-sleeved, wind-tunnel-tested, time trial skinsuits, which arrived just in time for the trip. And Fast Forward sent six new disc wheels and high-profile aero front wheels, rounding out everything the riders needed to go fast.

In August, the guys met up at the Feehery house in suburban Chicago to train. They assembled and tweaked the new bikes and rode as many miles as possible. Their part-time director, Wenger, was on hand to teach them the finer points of riding a tight rotation in various winds: communication, timing, and most importantly, concentration. The first few rides involved a lot of yelling and chaos, which was to be expected. With each bad rotation, awkward exchange, and near miss during the early training sessions, the very real potential for crashing the entire team became evident. That would have ended the project immediately.

The notion of preparing for the world championships stoked a different fire under each rider and led to some training rides that took the riders to new heights of focus and new depths of suffering. Gardner went so deep on one of the rides that he became wobbly on the bike. Wenger was forced to throw him into the team van mid-ride and transport him back to the house.

They also struggled to balance their different abilities. When Sitler pushed too hard on the hills, there were protests. There was more unhappiness when Silverberg rode them straight through the roughest section of road and when Gardner touched wheels with Cortlan in a crosswind. The dire warnings from the older riders about this team competing in the world championships were making sense. But one day during one of their hardest training runs, the group crested a hill and everything clicked into place. They achieved complete cycling bliss: a vacuous silence broken only by the scratchy whir of the disc wheels. Millimeters from one another in a perfect formation, they were flying down the road at 37 mph.

Suddenly, they believed they could beat some of the other American Continental teams, like Lupus, Jamis–Hagens Berman, and Champion System–Stan's NoTubes. After a few more good training sessions, they felt they were ready.

With no budget for flights, the riders drove themselves to Richmond. They stayed at a crummy hotel and ate at Chipotle, just as they did at many other races. Why change now?

When the Astellas van parked alongside the massive BMC and Cannondale team buses, it became clear that this was a case of David and Goliath. The team was unfazed and beyond excited to compete against the best in the sport.

At worlds, the entire 23-mile course, along with every cross street and side road, was closed to traffic on the day before the race so teams could pre-ride it. There was more fanfare and larger crowds for the pre-ride than the guys had seen at any race during the season. Fans lined the entire course. They didn't care if it was BMC, Team Sky, LottoNL-Jumbo, or Astellas Pro Cycling; they cheered for everyone. It was the most exciting non-race the Astellas riders had ever experienced.

The team pulled off the practice ride without incident. They made mental notes on how to tackle the technical course that wound its way in and around downtown Richmond. They occasionally had to reel in Silverberg when the cheering caused his adrenaline to pump at a higher rate, but they returned to the van confident and ready.

For Curin and Frey, the team managers' pre-race meeting was a surreal experience. They had a place at the table with WorldTour directors and a placard with their names on it—proof that both had come a long way from their Pharmacia days.

The next morning the riders awoke with surprisingly little nervousness. They felt ready. They simply needed to ride their bikes as fast as possible, turn where necessary, and not bump into each other.

The team handled the pre-race scene with aplomb. They didn't get starry-eyed when Peter Sagan rode past on his way to the porta-john, and they were nonchalant about using the same porta-john as Peter Sagan just moments after Peter Sagan. And so what if their bikes didn't match and no one knew their names? Astellas was holding the lowest spot on the totem pole, but they were on the totem pole.

In the distance, the crowd surrounding the starting line was cheering. Every few minutes, the familiar chirp of the countdown clock wafted over to remind them that they were on a critical path. Everything was going perfectly until the curse of being a small budget team struck . . . twice.

Fast Forward had asked Frey if he could loan one of their FFWD disc wheels to one of the women's teams that the company was also sponsoring for their race. He was assured that the team would return it in time for the men's start, and Frey had agreed. Now, just minutes before the men's race, the wheel still hadn't been returned. The only spare wheels available were heavy-duty aluminum training wheels with clincher tires, so Jake Silverberg was forced to put those on his bike.

Then, during the bike inspection, which takes place 15 minutes before the start, Cortlan's bike was deemed out of compliance. In assembling the bike, he had mounted handlebars that extended too far forward by two centimeters. Since he had never used his TT bike in competition, it had never been properly inspected. Seeing as how it was worlds, the UCI commissaires weren't going to let it slide. The bike was deemed noncompliant.

WorldTour team bikes are inspected multiple times during the course of the season, and every team has a fully equipped repair facility in their truck and a stable of spare bikes standing by in case of emergency. The Astellas van, however, was virtually empty. There were very few tools and the riders didn't bring spare bikes, so Frey and Bavolar tried every way they could think of to pull the bike back into compliance. Bavolar scrambled around fruitlessly looking for a hacksaw to cut down the bars. As the clock ticked down to the official start, Frey came close to asking other American teams if they had a spare bike, but he decided against it.

The frantic search was raising anxiety in the Astellas camp. Without a bike, Cortlan would be forced to sit out. The rest of the team was warming up on stationary trainers, watching their team of six become a team of five.

Meanwhile, Bavolar was instructed by UCI inspectors to put electrical tape over the logos on the Ritchey handlebars and stems because they contained small graphics of rainbow stripes, which under UCI rules are reserved for current or former world champions. The debacle was a momentary distraction from the chaos caused by the noncompliant handlebars.

Had the team carried a spare road bike to Richmond, even one that wasn't set up for a time trial, Cortlan could line up at the start and contribute something for the first few miles.

At the last possible minute, a dejected Cortlan climbed into the team van and removed his helmet. He wouldn't be racing today.

As the team mounted the steps into the start house, the mechanic from the women's team sauntered over to return the borrowed FFWD disc wheel. In the pre race chaos, the team had neglected to scavenge Cortlan's bike, so they frantically swapped out Silverberg's heavy training wheel for the faster disc wheel in the start house.

The clock ticked down to zero. The team rocketed out onto the course and quickly settled into the rhythm they had rehearsed in Chicago. All the pre-race chaos melted away into a concentrated ride through a blurry tunnel. They didn't see or hear the crowd, and they didn't think about it being the world championships. They simply turned the pedals and kept their respective noses out of the wind for the next 20 miles. Another mechanical issue arose and Gardner and Feehery struggled with slipping saddles on the new time trial bikes, but they weren't going to let it destroy their ride.

With UCI rules requiring only four riders to finish, the team followed their plan and let Silverberg pull them, with his final pull taking them to the bottom of the climb on Governor Street. His effort was remarkable and caused the other four to hang on for dear life. They approached the turn onto Governor like a commuter train, and when Silverberg peeled off, it became Sitler's job to lead them up the hill.

On the Governor Street climb, noise from the largest crowd on the course hit them like a shock wave and they picked up speed. It was a surreal feeling for each of them, and in that instant, Gardner reflected on how far he had come since that sketchy night in New York, when he first landed in the United States. Barreling down the finishing straight, a rush of emotion swept over him. Bombarded with cheers from the crowd and thoughts of everything that conspired to put him in this place—the support of his family, Green's recommendation, the Dave Rayner Fund's financial backing—the actual riding became secondary. Then he snapped back to reality and put everything he had into the last 500 meters.

Jenkins had raced in big events before. The Amgen Tour of California has huge crowds and big-name stars, so this was nothing new. But he also felt a similar wave of emotion as he crossed the finish line. He was proud of what the team was able to accomplish under the circumstances and in such a short time. He also felt a deep sense of personal accomplishment at having reached this point, knowing full well that it might be the highlight of his career.

Astellas rolled across the line completely spent and near the bottom of the standings. But they had done it. They competed at the world championships. They escaped humiliation and they didn't crash. They suffered no ride-halting mechanical issues on the course, and while they hadn't beaten any of the other Continental teams, they were happy to have gone to Richmond.

As it turned out, they didn't finish in last place. Elsewhere on the course, two members of the Tinkoff-Saxo team had crashed when

Michael Rogers and Michael Valgren touched wheels. They lost time regrouping and finished a couple of minutes behind Astellas. It was inconsequential to the team; there was no moral victory in another team's misfortune.

The trip to worlds was a microcosm of the team's existence. Severely underfunded and woefully understaffed, they made mistakes, but they looked the part, tried like hell, and came out better for having endured. It was the pinnacle of the team's existence thus far.

Even this near-last place finish would be hard to top.

CHAPTER 16

CYCLING'S CLEAR AND PRESENT DANGER

One of the biggest dangers in the sport of cycling isn't the bike race itself. From curbside, a race can seem chaotic. It looks like the entire peloton could crash at any moment. In reality, it is a ballet of coordinated motion like a school of fish or a flock of birds turning and flowing together, barring the occasional pileup.

The real danger is in the preparation. Cycling (and to a lesser degree, triathlon) is the only sport in which the athletes must train out on the open road alongside motor vehicle traffic. According to a majority of motorists, cyclists should find a sidewalk or bike path to ride on far from traffic. That's not the least bit feasible. There is no other reasonable option to train for the sport of bike racing than to ride on public roadways.

It is the worst part of the sport.

Most cyclists develop a sixth sense about safety. They can look at a road and make a snap decision about its ridability. By riding so many thousands of miles each year, they gain a deeper understanding of driver behavior and will seek out the quietest roads with the most challenging terrain. Very few serious cyclists care about scenery or the weather. It's seldom a pleasure cruise.

Conversely, some riders give it no thought whatsoever and will ride on any paved surface stretched between points A and B. This type of rider lumps all roads into one category and places a great amount of faith in the belief that all drivers have their wits about them. They may have grown up in a part of the world where cyclists are given equal standing. America is not counted among the bike-friendly countries. Granted, some regions are better than others. Overall, though, it's a crap shoot.

When Matt Green gets on his bike, he is very conscious of the route he takes. He's concerned for his own safety and that of his fellow riders and even motorists. He understands how cyclists are perceived, and he understands what one bike on a road can do to traffic patterns. As a result, he looks for quiet roads where traffic is light and where, if he does see a car, the driver is less distracted by other stimuli.

Rural Pennsylvania may have some of the best cycling roads in the country. Away from the major metropolises of Pittsburgh and Phila-delphia, the roads are smooth, twisty, and hilly, and the countryside is scenic. Away from those cities, "traffic" is just the name of a rock band from the 1970s, and "rush hour" is a Jackie Chan movie. In the southeast corner of the state, the bucolic Pennsylvania Dutch farms stretch out for miles in every direction over the rolling hills.

Green was on a normal training ride on one of those lovely country roads in the middle of nowhere, preparing for the 2015 Philadelphia International Cycling Classic in early June. Astellas team members often stayed at Sitler's house in nearby Marietta, Pennsylvania, using it as a base of operations during the season for races on the east coast. The Sitler family owns a convenience store in town, and Jake's parents loved having the team stay with them.

A light rain started to fall as Matt was in the final miles of a 70-mile ride. As he descended a long hill he saw a car ahead start to pull out and then hesitate. Matt guessed that the driver saw him approaching, so he continued, still going pretty fast but paying attention. As he closed in, the car suddenly turned into Matt's lane. Matt swerved to avoid a collision but struck the front quarter panel with his left side.

He was taken out in an instant.

Green lay on the road in a crumpled heap. He awoke to find a man kneeling over him, applying a tourniquet to his leg. Were it not for the driver's quick action, the outcome would have been catastrophic.

Worried about making a mess in the ambulance, Green asked the driver to take it easy because he didn't want to get carsick, but puking was the least of his problems. The medical report was horrific. He had broken every bone in his left leg. Twice. He had also broken his back, collarbone, and arm. His femoral artery was torn. And his hair was mussed up pretty badly.

When the doctor attempted to straighten out his left leg prior to surgery, Green passed out from the pain. It was just the beginning.

His girlfriend, Tracy, flew in from Milwaukee the next day. Sitler's mother and his fiancé, Jamie, were also at Green's side every day as he struggled through tidal waves of pain. The pain medication was putting up a meager fight. The only silver lining was the fact that the crash happened near the Sitlers' hometown, which allowed them to visit frequently.

GREEN LOVED CYCLING. It was his life's calling from an early age and all he really knew outside school and family. As he lay in the hospital bed day after day, he knew that at 27, he was not ready to give up racing. Despite the medical report that spanned several pages and a team of doctors suggesting he might never walk again, he knew he would race again. When he verbalized that to Tracy and his teammates, they reacted with the customary supportive agreement, yet no one fully believed it. Not in the first several days, anyway. He was loopy, for one thing, and his body was held together by pins, screws, and bungee cords. And every day spent in the hospital bed would cause his muscles to atrophy further.

But his bones began healing immediately, and, in his mind, the road to recovery started the moment that he hit the pavement.

He spent almost three weeks in the Pennsylvania hospital and was given tremendous care by the staff, Tracy, and the Sitlers. His father flew in from England. Teammates made the trip to his hospital room to offer their support. Those that couldn't visit in person sent emails of encouragement and concern. Cortlan and his wife Amber sent candy, and Green's guests helped themselves. Because he was unable to sit up to eat his meals due to the pain, the Sitlers kept his hospital room fully stocked with Goldfish and Sprite. It was all he could handle.

Clay Murfet hand-delivered a pair of socks.

Pactimo had sent a new shipment of socks to the team, and Murfet wanted to make sure that a pair made it into Green's hands. The gesture meant a lot to Green, and those socks were a reminder that his team was behind him. It would take several months to get to the point where he could actually put them on, but he kept them nearby nonetheless.

Out of the blue, Green received a call from Jeff Fulford, the team's host in Redlands, California, who wanted to offer his professional advice on physical therapy to help Matt recover.

It was gut-wrenching for the guys to see their teammate in this condition. They were like brothers. One by one, they would walk into his room, get the report, hear the prognosis, see him wrapped in various bandages and braces, and do their best to bolster his spirits.

It's impossible for a cyclist to visit another cyclist in the hospital and not blanch at the uncomfortable realization that "this could happen to me." At any time on any training ride or in any bike race, a severe crash can put a rider into a scenario like the one Green was struggling through. And it's normal to ask the question: Is it worth the risk?

Cycling is an absolute blast, and though it is a high-risk sport, the likelihood of being in an accident is quite low. In most situations, riders can, to a certain degree, mitigate the effects of a crash. They can swerve, brake, bunny-hop, or otherwise lessen the impact of an impending crash. But every now and then, a driver jukes one way and goes the other, and tragedy strikes. Every rider knows this can happen. But they sometimes file it away too deeply.

WHEN GREEN WAS DISCHARGED, his father drove him home to Milwaukee. Of all the long drives Green had made across the States, his 15-hour car ride to Wisconsin was far and away the worst. Still in terrible pain, he could likely estimate with great accuracy how many concrete seams and potholes there are on I-80 between Pittsburgh and Chicago. Every single jolt left its mark.

They arrived in Milwaukee just in time for the Waukesha stage of the Tour of America's Dairyland. TOAD was the original inspiration behind Green's decision to stay in the States and continue racing criteriums. It was his Yankee Stadium—the place where he felt the most at home in a bike race. Hobbling the 100 feet from the car to the racecourse with his walker took several minutes.

His teammates were thrilled to have Green at the race, and they were intent on turning out a solid performance in his honor. Gardner and Feehery made it into a breakaway that lapped the field. Monk won the sprint.

As Green watched the awards ceremony, he promised himself that he would be racing in Waukesha one year hence.

Despite losing the entire 2015 season, Green was guaranteed a spot on the team for 2016. Curin and Frey believed he could make a comeback and felt that his loyalty to the team deserved the opportunity. They knew the medical prognosis and were willing to accept it as truth, but they also knew that they owed Green the chance to prove it wrong.

CHAPTER 17

UNCERTAINTY SETS IN

In November, Astellas corporate notified Curin and Frey that 2016 would be its last season as sponsor. The company was changing direction and had trimmed its marketing budget; the cycling team was expendable. Curin was crestfallen but powerless to change the decision. With more funds budgeted than previous years, they went ahead with plans for 2016 to include a 16-person roster, divided into criterium and road squads, as they had done in 2015. And they would immediately ramp up their efforts to find a new title sponsor for the team for the following year.

With Myerson now retired, the criterium squad needed a new mentor. Frey invited Aldo Ino Ilesic, a Slovenian strongman who had ridden for United Healthcare and Team Type 1, and more recently with the Austrian-based Team Vorarlberg. Ilesic was looking for an American team to ride crits with to stay in shape for Red Hook events, a series of criterium-like races ridden on fixed gear bikes and a tight course. Red Hook had become wildly popular, not strictly for its tactical subtleties but for its brute force and thrilling speeds. The series began in 2008 as a single event in the Red Hook neighborhood of Brooklyn, New York, and quickly attracted an enthusiastic, if not bloodthirsty, following drawn to a race known for the massive pileups that are bound to happen when racing brakeless bikes around narrow city streets at night.

Through his Red Hook contract with Specialized, Ilesic brought the manufacturer on board as the Astellas bike sponsor. Each rider would be provided with an aluminum frame, which caught the team by surprise: Aluminum had been popular in the 1990s, until carbon fiber became the material of choice for race bikes. But aluminum was making a comeback, and Specialized, like competitors Trek and Cannondale, began to promote its revived aluminum offering. Bike sponsors often equip teams with their high-end carbon fiber bikes and the latest gadgetry, but Specialized wanted to demonstrate that it had a bike at an affordable price point ($2,000—cheap compared to higher-end carbon fiber bikes) that could win races and withstand the rigors of travel.

They were right. The bikes were fast and nimble, and they could take a ding to the tubing that would otherwise ruin a carbon fiber frame.

Specialized would also provide the time trial specialists with its high-end Shiv time trial bikes. One rider who would appreciate the bike was a new recruit, David Williams. Entering his seventh pro season, Williams came from the Jamis–Hagens Berman team. He had the same type of stage-racing experience as Jenkins: the Amgen Tour of California, the Larry H. Miller Tour of Utah, and the USA Pro Challenge in Colorado. He had won the bronze medal at the national time trial championships in 2014 and 2015, and now his entire focus was to win gold in 2016.

Williams had spent the winter in intense training mode. Specialized brought him into their wind tunnel and helped refine his riding position, which gave him the confidence that he had lacked at his previous teams. Finally, he felt that he also had the support he needed.

Eamon Lucas and Ian Keough were added to the crit squad. Keough was the youngest of five racing brothers (the others are Jake, Nick, Luke, and Jesse) from Sandwich, Massachusetts. Keough was a quiet, reserved 18-year-old. Lucas was the exact opposite: larger than life, a

California surfer with a heart of gold, who listens to hip-hop and rap at a volume of 10. Sometimes 11. Lucas had trained as a member of the USAC's national team program and had lived in the USAC house in Europe until he aged out of the program in 2014. He rode for another small Continental team in 2015. He brought an energy to the team that outsiders often misunderstood and probably resented. In his mind, life is a party to be enjoyed, not a sentence to be endured. Over time, his crit teammates came to appreciate his boundless energy and infectious laugh.

Frey found a national champion to add to the roster in 19-year-old Olly Moors, the recently crowned British National Derny Champion. A friend of Green and Gardner, he came to the team via the Dave Rayner Fund, which had also made Gardner's spot on the team possible. Moors's confidence belied his age—a strength he'd need in his move stateside. He would find America and American cycling to be an adjustment, but he quickly came to love racing criteriums.

Young riders Johnathan Freter and Ansel Dickey also joined the road squad. Freter, 24, already had a lot of racing in his legs from two years spent with the Jelly Belly team. Twenty-year-old Dickey, a former ski racer from Killington, Vermont, had been coached as a junior by East Coast stalwart Peter Vollers. Dickey's current coach, Joe Holmes, brought him to Frey's attention.

Dickey came to the team injured. A poor bike fit resulted in muscular imbalance in his hips and a misaligned kneecap, which led to an inflamed IT band. His season never quite got off the ground.

Travis Livermon was the last rider added to the roster. Nationally ranked as a cyclocross racer, he had spent four years with the Smart-Stop Conti team. Myerson recommended him strongly. Livermon could add strength to the road squad while using the training and racing to help his cyclocross career in the way Hyde had in 2014 and 2015.

Frey felt he had a strong mix of riders heading into the 2016 season: promising youth and experienced veterans. Looking ahead another year or two, this was a team that could line up at the Amgen Tour of California or Larry H. Miller Tour of Utah. It all hinged on finding a sponsor to sustain what they had going for them.

WHILE THE NEW RIDERS signed on, the team was also getting settled financially. In December, Astellas made the sponsorship official and sent their initial payment in the form of a check for $350,000—70 percent of the $500,000 contract—to Frey's Cycling Development Foundation. Frey moved forward with plans for the racing season. The budget was larger than the previous season's, so Frey had reason to be excited about the team's season.

But just a month later, Astellas would exercise its option to terminate the relationship and stop payment in 30 days. This is a call that all cycling team directors dread, but many have had to take. Some go to war with the sponsor. Some sneak out the back door without saying goodbye or paying their bills. Frey could only accept the decision with the obligatory, "Thank you for all you've done for us."

The team was dejected, depressed, demoralized. They understood how the business end of the sport worked and that Astellas's decision was well within their rights. But still they felt disgusted with the state of the sport in general and its reliance upon a funding framework that doesn't truly work. It was the bane of cycling's existence, and now their lives were directly affected by it.

Frey immediately focused on getting the most out of the season. He had already committed more money in rider salaries for the new year. If he was unable to change the salary structure, the shortfall would cut into the team's travel and race registrations.

Registration fees for races such as the Tour of America's Dairyland cost $4,500 for the six-man team. A full season of transportation, food, and housing costs two arms and a leg. Paying the riders to race wouldn't work if they couldn't afford to go anywhere. However, paying the riders nothing but asking them to race a full schedule wouldn't be fair to the riders. Frey had to find a balance.

He gave them two options: the riders could take their salary in full and walk away, or they could ride as a team, spend the money until it was gone, and hope that a new sponsor would keep the team alive.

The best bet was to take the check and walk away.

The riders agreed to ride out the season for as long as the money would last. They wanted to race as a team. Even before they had met, they saw a strong roster with great potential. Being bike racers in love with their sport, they took the gamble and trusted that Frey was diligent in his sponsor search.

He was indeed diligent. But it was bike racing, after all. A tough sell.

SPRING WASN'T ALL DOWNCAST. In late February, before the American season even began, the European racing season kicked off, and the Astellas team had something to cheer about.

During the season opener, Omloop Het Nieuwsblad, almost the entire Astellas team was tuned in via the Internet, and it might have been one of the proudest moments for the team. Their former teammate Brecht Dhaene was in the breakaway.

Brecht had moved back to Belgium in the off-season and signed on with the Belgian Pro Continental team Verandas Willems. By virtue of being a European Continental team, his team was eligible to race in many of the classics. And now, there he was, off the front in the first well-known race of the season.

The Astellas riders were messaging back and forth while the race played out. They were encouraging him from afar. And urging him not to whip out his camera and take any selfies.

Bike racers can be cruel.

Brecht had been in the early 12-man breakaway for much of the first part of the race. Peter Sagan and Greg Van Avermaet and a couple of others went across the gap, joined the breakaway briefly, and then started dropping the members of the original group. Brecht hung in for quite a while before finally dropping. He finished in 26th place.

For the Astellas riders, it was amazing to see a former teammate and friend riding in a breakaway with reigning world champion Sagan. The move to a European Conti team could be considered a lateral move, but it put Brecht in position to race many more high-profile events that he wasn't getting to race in the States.

Brecht's appearance in the breakaway was a milestone for the Astellas team. While the crit squad measured its success with a tally of wins and podium appearances, the road squad did so by the advancement of its riders. Here was pixelated proof of the team's success.

MANY OF THE SAME SPONSORS returned for the 2016 season. Pactimo brought a slightly new kit design with them, adding a section of black to the bodice that strengthened the look without detracting from the Red Army image. It was a clean design that they hoped to carry across the finish line.

3T signed on as the new handlebar and stem sponsor. Ritchey provided saddles and other components. Soigneur came back for another season, providing embrocation and chamois cream. Clif Bar, Tifosi, and Northwave each contributed to the stone soup. The team headed into the new season ready to leave its mark.

CHAPTER 18

SEASON 5: RED AND BLACK

The division between the Astellas criterium squad and the Astellas road squad was evident right away. The chemistry that the crit squad had developed over the previous season carried over and proved stronger than any cohesion going on across the aisle. When Ilesic acquired kits exclusively for the crit guys, the gap widened. Because Pactimo was inundated with orders from amateur clubs throughout the country, they were unable to get the team's kits delivered in time for the early-season criteriums. Ilesic used his Specialized contacts to secure bikes for the entire team, along with some black-and-red Specialized kits for the crit squad so that they wouldn't have to cobble together kits from the previous year or buy their own. The gesture created an undertone of resentment with some of the roadies that bubbled under the surface for most of the year.

Prior to the season's start, Frey decided that a second van was needed to help stretch the smaller budget. He bought a used Dodge Sprinter van similar to the white Mercedes Sprinter, only this one was an ugly shade of green. The unmarked vehicle was given to the crit squad, who quickly dubbed it the "creeper van." It was reconfigured to carry bikes, wheels, and bags by ripping out the rearmost seat and bolting a bunch of two-by-fours together. It looked like hell, but it worked.

Although it had more than 250,000 miles on the odometer, it drove well, and by this time, the team had given up on the idea of traveling in style.

Having Ilesic and David Williams on board boosted the team's credibility and hinted at an increase in budget and staff, but behind the scenes it was still a one-man crew running a full slate of freelancers: a soigneur here, a mechanic or a driver there, maybe a team director.

Cash-strapped, Frey frequently called in favors from his friends to fill any remaining gaps. Gus Carillo, Joe Holmes, and David Wenger were accustomed to working for various teams throughout the year, for a month, a weekend, or a single day. They served as plug-and-play solutions for Astellas. Any one of them could fly to a race such as Philly or Joe Martin, slot themselves into any team's car for a day, and manage a race without ever having met any of the riders. They brought the same dedication and work ethic regardless of which team they represented on a given weekend.

Carillo had experience working with United Healthcare and other pro teams. He had raced with the Guiltless Gourmet team in the 1990s and knew the various races and racecourses around the country. As a race director, his usual mode of operation was very low stress. He knew that wasted energy was lost forever.

Joe Holmes worked with the Astellas team, Garneau-Quebecor, and a handful of others. When Gus or Joe weren't available, David Wenger was usually available and willing.

Team mechanics are also interchangeable, and the Astellas team utilized a handful of wrenches throughout their five-year run. Kelley was their mainstay mechanic, who had come to them through the team's partnership with the Goodspeed Bike Shop. Gary Bavolar filled in at big events, including the world championships. Erik Hamilton also spent time with the team off and on. But with two teams traveling extensively in 2016, they decided to hire a full-time mechanic to keep things working smoothly.

A team mechanic isn't critical at a single-day criterium. If something breaks during the race, it can be handled in the neutral support pit area by whomever is on hand. And, even though it would be handy for Astellas's crit squad to have a mechanic at a series like TOAD where the bikes often take a beating (and neutral support mechanics are busy fixing other people's problems), there is enough down time between races for riders to find a local bike shop or fix it themselves. Mechanics are more valuable at stage races such as the Redlands Classic. With six riders racing three road races, a time trial, and a criterium, the equipment requires extra attention to be ready each day.

When the team arrived at the Fulfords' house in Redlands, they met their new mechanic, who had arrived a day early to get started assembling the time trial bikes. He had worked as a freelancer with other teams and came highly recommended by friends in the industry.

On the operational front, the team organization was playing catchup at Redlands. A late start in getting things rolling in January meant that many of the riders hadn't received their clothing. Helmets were still in boxes. Some riders hadn't built their time trial bikes yet. So the scene in the Fulfords' driveway was even more chaotic than normal as equipment was sorted and assembled and clothing was distributed.

On agreeing to wrench for Astellas, the mechanic spent a few weeks outfitting the van to his liking. An air compressor installed into the vehicle made tire inflation easier. Racks for 18 bikes and dozens of spare wheels were installed, although after just one cross-country trip they were looking the worse for wear. Storage space for accessories was limited, and nothing was labeled yet. The rear seat of the Mercedes van had been removed to make room for the time trial bikes, which made the passenger space smaller. It was cozy.

Things got off to a friendly start as the team organized their equipment, but there was an unmistakable tension building by the hour. All this should have been squared away long before they arrived in California, not on the eve of the biggest race on the calendar. The team tried to remain understanding. Everything would be fine as long as the time trial specialists and G.C. contenders had enough time to get their bikes dialed in. The rest of the riders could tweak their bikes in preparation for the time trial on stage 2.

The first stage of Redlands is a circuit race on a course in the neighboring town of Highland, California. It featured one large uphill stretch and a long descent through the local neighborhood. It turned out to be a disaster. Drywall screws were showing up in tires everywhere. Freter had a flat tire in the first mile and never regained contact with the field. He failed to make the time cut and sat out the rest of the weekend. David Williams suffered two flat tires and just barely made the time cut to advance to the second stage. Jenkins was the top finisher in 21st.

That night, the mechanic had his hands full with rims, tires, and glue. When he texted photos from an L.A. nightclub at 1 a.m., the team assumed he was ahead of the game.

He wasn't. The next morning, riders discovered that he had only repaired half of the wheels. They'd have to rely on neutral support.

Stage 2, with its mountain finish at Oak Glen, wasn't much better. The best the team could muster was Sitler's 37th place, more than a minute behind stage winner Sepp Kuss, one of the young up-and-comers from Chris Creed's Gateway Harley-Davidson team.

Arriving at the time trial venue on day three, morale was starting to tank. A rainy morning didn't help. As the riders began to unload the van, they immediately noticed that the pedals had been removed from each of the time trial bikes. Before the team was able to find him, the mechanic hopped in the team's rental car and drove back to the host family's garage nine miles away to retrieve them, but the damage was irreversible. Without pedals, the riders couldn't warm up. Frey was forced to do the walk of shame from one team van to the next, asking if anyone had extra pedals to loan to him. It was a fruitless search.

Olly Moors would be the first rider to start by virtue of holding the lowest place, 147th. His time trial bike wasn't affected by the pedal problem because it was still in a cardboard box, unassembled, so he rode his standard road bike. David Williams wasn't so lucky. He was the team's best hope in the time trial. If any bike should have been ready, it was his.

Before the time trial was over, Frey decided he had seen enough. He called Curin in Chicago to relay the fiasco and its profound impact on the team's performance. While the team struggled through the time trial, Curin hurriedly made arrangements to fly the mechanic home later that night.

When they returned from the race, Frey broke the news to the mechanic who angrily threw some things out of the van and onto the Fulfords' lawn, opened the property gate, and drove out with tires squealing. Both bumpers scraped on the steep driveway, setting off a spray of sparks.

The team was angry about how carelessly their equipment was handled, both at the race and now as he bolted from the scene. They were even more livid that he had driven off without closing the property gate behind him—a house rule that the team was careful to uphold. Had Montana gotten out, things would have turned even more ugly. They hadn't been riding well to begin with, and now they were burdened with the task of loading the van, taking inventory, making repairs, and cleaning up the mess left behind, all while apologizing profusely to the Fulfords.

Frey faced the unenviable task of retrieving team equipment, including the van's rear seat and several spare wheels, from the disgruntled freelancer's garage on the other side of the country. The exchange would take months to sort out.

Saturday's criterium in downtown Redlands was relatively uneventful until the final turn on the final lap. Monk, who years earlier had learned to be among the first five riders through the final corner, came through the turn in perfect position to launch his sprint, but two riders from the Silber team tumbled in front of him, causing a massive pileup of at least 20 riders. Monk was the first to take flight. He landed on his head and shoulder and immediately feared a broken collarbone. Nothing was broken, but it was another disappointing outing in a weekend full of disappointment.

The team made it through the rest of the Redlands Classic with Sitler as their most successful rider in 34th place overall, more than five minutes behind the winner, Canadian Matteo Dal-Cin of the Silber team.

The riders couldn't wait to put Redlands in the rearview mirror. The disastrous weekend, combined with turmoil over sponsorship, was weighing heavily on every rider. It was the beginning of the end for the road squad, and it wasn't yet April.

MEANWHILE, ON THE OTHER SIDE of the country, the guys in the creeper van were winning money. Ilesic was a dominating force in early-season criteriums. At 6'3" and 200 pounds, his size made him an imposing figure in a fast-moving criterium field. After finishing fifth overall in the National Criterium Calendar in 2015, he swore off road racing for good. He loved crits and wanted to teach younger riders how to win them.

Astellas returned to Athens, Georgia, with Ilesic in tow, ready to race Twilight and erase any lingering memories of the calamity in 2014. Sometimes teams will skip a race if they had bad luck there previously, but Twilight is not to be missed. Every rider has something bad to say about Twilight as they're pinning on their race number.

The field was 170 riders strong at the start of the race. With so many riders stretched around a 1-kilometer course, a breakaway doesn't have to get very far off the front before it catches the rear of the pack.

Ryan Aitcheson and Eamon Lucas lapped the field with five other riders. When they caught the back of the pack, Murfet, Monk, and Ilesic escorted them to the front of the field to wait for another attack. Just a few laps later, another breakaway formed during a prime sprint, and it included one of the original escapees: Oscar Clark (Holowesko-Citadel). Ilesic saw the danger of letting Clark get away on such a short course, so he dragged Aitcheson and four others across the gap to join them. Taking Bobby Lea (Maloja Pushbikers), another rider from the early breakaway along, Ilesic's pack gained a lap. Now Clark, Lea, and Aitcheson were two laps ahead, while Ilesic, Eamon, and a handful of others were just one lap ahead.

Twilight is sensory overload for young riders. Riders are dropping out at a high rate, and breakaways lap the field multiple times carrying different riders with them each time. With its short, fast course, dancing shadows, loud crowd, thumping music, and a huge field that never slows down, communication is critical yet nearly impossible. If a team can race without talking, they hold the advantage.

Over the final 15 laps, Eamon, Monk, and Murfet knew what to do. They formed a red train on the front and rotated along at a pace that prevented anyone from attacking. Ilesic and Aitcheson sat in fourth and fifth position. Astellas was in complete control of one of America's "monument" races. The rest of the team was watching the livestream and loving what they saw. The Red Army was holding the position traditionally played by the United Healthcare Blue Train or the Optum–Kelly Benefits orange train, controlling the last laps.

With just over four laps remaining, Eamon and Monk each took one final pull and dropped out, completely spent. Murfet drilled it with Ilesic and Aitcheson tucked in behind him. The rest of the field—by now whittled down to just 50 riders—lined up in Aitcheson's draft, content to let the red train do all the work. With two laps to go, Holowesko-Citadel sent two riders to the front: Andzs Flaksis and Clark. With one lap to go, two riders from Lea's Maloja Pushbikers team took over the lead. As the bell rang, Ilesic looked over his shoulder to make sure Aitcheson was right behind him and pointed to his own rear wheel, as if Aitcheson needed to be reminded. He didn't. He was ready.

On the back stretch, Ilesic took over with a blistering lead-out into the final two turns, and Aitcheson held on tight. Gaps were opening up between him and his two opponents, Clark and Lea. He sprinted past Ilesic and crossed the line as the winner. Ilesic finished in fourth place.

It was the biggest win ever scored by the team. They avoided the fates that dictated their past results, and raced it perfectly from beginning to end.

HAVING HAD NO TRAINING CAMP in the spring, the national championship weekend in Winston-Salem was the first and only time the two squads met all year. It was also the first chance for either squad to see how the other was traveling. The crit squad was furious to find out that the white sprinter van was so lavishly stocked with expendables such as new chains, tires, wheels, and cables when they had been buying their own stuff at bike shops with their own money and waiting to be reimbursed. Because the crit squad had been winning money quite regularly, they felt they deserved better support. But for Frey it was merely a problem of logistics. With two squads traveling in different directions, making sure both groups had what they needed in relatively equal supply was a huge challenge.

Equipment was strewn across the yard at Travis Livermon's house in Winston-Salem as the two squads settled their differences and redistributed the wealth. Looking ahead to the next month of races, they decided that more seating was needed in the white Sprinter van, so they took the backseat from the crit squad's van and strapped it down using cargo straps. It wobbled, but it would have to do.

Once everything was sorted, the two squads were good to go.

Heading into nationals, David Williams had something to prove. His entire season and career hinged on his time trial ride. He resolved to use a good result to climb to a Pro Continental team or look to life after cycling. He had no desire to continue living at the whim of fickle sponsors. Problem was, he was coming off a demoralizing ride at the Tour of the Gila where Tom Zirbel had taken almost a full minute out of him on a 17-mile course. Nationals proved to be no easier on his psyche, as Taylor Phinney beat a strong Zirbel by over a minute, a result that would cause even the strongest time trialists to question their career choice. David finished in eighth place, more than two minutes behind.

Johnathan Freter also hoped to do well in the time trial. A meticulous rider, he had painstakingly adjusted his bike trying to milk more speed out of it. He was unable to finish due to an ill-timed flat far from neutral support.

Eamon Lucas pulled a solid 10th-place finish, less than a minute behind David Williams; it was a great result for a crit specialist in a time trial.

In the road race, the team missed every decisive move and never mustered enough effort to regain contact with the leaders. It wasn't a particularly tough course, but the heat and humidity winnowed the field down to just 25 finishers. Sitler finished in 22nd place.

Unhappy but pushing on, the roadies hopped into the white van the next day and drove to the Philadelphia Classic, where Sitler managed to finish in 20th place. Jenkins was 50th. Dan Gardner didn't finish the race, but he left town feeling that he had found his place in the sport; he liked the challenge that Philly had presented him.

A lack of cohesion was undermining the road squad. Some riders were competing more as individuals, chasing top placings to help pay for the season through winnings. And others rode as individuals in search of the one big win that would land them a spot on a new team. It was a difficult way for a team to race.

Leaving Philadelphia, the team continued driving north to Quebec for the Grand Prix Cycliste de Saguenay. Stage 1 showcased 151 wet kilometers. The team was in disarray, but Gardner was riding well. The young British rider hadn't been eligible to race in the US National Championships and didn't finish Philly, so he was somewhat fresh and eager to race, pulling off an impressive 17th-place finish.

In the stage 3 criterium, Travis Livermon made it into a breakaway of 11 riders that formed off the front. Knowing that the other 10 riders were preparing for a sprint finish, he threw a wrench into the works and attacked early, got a gap, and held off the thundering herd for a solo victory. In terms of the prize, it was the best result for the road squad all year, and another ironic criterium win for the roadies.

Stage 4 was another cold and rainy slog: 14 circuits of a 6-mile course containing a long climb up an 8 percent grade with steeper sections topping out at 20 percent. Very few North American races include gradients so steep. In fact, very few roads are that steep. Nearly half of the 94-man field would drop out before gutting out all 14 climbs.

Dickey, Green, Livermon, and Williams each cut their race short and retreated to the van. But Gardner was enjoying the torture. This was the type of race he had been waiting for. He thought the Philly race was one that he could eventually win, and the final stage of Saguenay felt vaguely similar. The climb was longer and tougher than Philly's Manayunk Wall, which suited Dan's skillset.

He stayed with the lead group on the climb on every lap, allowing just a few riders to break away. Meanwhile, he watched as other strong riders who had dropped him at previous races were disappearing off the back in silent agony. He competently handled the descent as others lost ground because of nerves.

Gardner crossed the line with a group of 20 riders, finishing 11th, just 34 seconds behind the winner. It was his best result with Astellas. His teammates were struck by the change in his demeanor. He had broken through an invisible wall at Saguenay and emerged with significantly more confidence on the bike, having realized that if he could survive that race, he could survive anything. Gardner would look back on the weekend in Quebec as the point when he became a full-fledged bike racer. The moral victory belonged to Frey, Curin, and Green, who had seen something special in Gardner right from the start.

Most spectators, and even most bike racers, would look at an 11th-place finish as just okay. But not every rider in every race is there to win it. Some are just trying to break through a wall to see what's on the other side. Others are trying to simply find the wall.

Shortly after Saguenay, Dan joined an amateur team in Belgium: Baguet-MIBA. By the end of 2016, he would be racing at the Continental Pro level again for An Post–Chain Reaction, a team supported by cycling legend Sean Kelly. His advancement was counted as another success for the road squad.

GREEN'S RETURN BOLSTERED everyone's spirits for the annual trip to TOAD. In truth, Green was still recovering from his crash a year earlier, and the various hardware holding his bones together made it difficult to race at 100 percent. In fact, his left leg was producing just 30 percent of its normal power, and every day brought a new pain as the pins and screws shifted about. But the team was happy to have him racing again, and it showed.

Monk had a string of second-place finishes that gave him enough points to put him in the race leader's jersey, which is not the customary yellow. At the Tour of America's Dairyland, the race leader's jersey is black and white and patterned like a Holstein.

Eamon won the Waukesha crit thanks to Green's massive lead-out on the final lap. It was an emotional victory for the team, as it marked a full year since a bandaged Green had hobbled to the curb to watch the team race.

Something trivial happened at the Port Washington stage of TOAD. Between turns one and two, there is a hill on Wisconsin Street as it passes the power plant. On that hill, a local rider had created a Strava KOM segment, which means that the online tracking app, Strava, was keeping track of everyone's individual efforts on the climb every single time they rode up it and ranking them according to whose time was the fastest. Since almost every pro bike racer uses a GPS unit to capture data from their training rides and races, they show up on the leaderboard. It is probably the best way for a cycling fan or amateur cyclist to measure their own abilities against faster riders like the pros racing at TOAD.

When the Astellas team was attempting to chase down the break-away in Port Washington, they put three riders on the front of the pack and stepped on the gas. They rode up the 600-meter hill gaining 100 feet in elevation in 51 seconds, putting them atop the leaderboard on Strava.

Pro riders will tell you that they don't really pay attention to things like that. And that is a lie. They may not track every Strava segment they ride, because it would take too much time, but they are well aware of the important KOM segments, especially if someone (namely another pro rider) steals it from them. For at least 2 years, Eamon, Murfet, and Green sat atop the KOM leaderboard on the vaunted Port Washington climb.

THE SEASON WAS WINDING DOWN. The road squad had moved on with their lives after Saguenay. Meanwhile, the crit squad was winning enough money to pay for the rest of their season. They kept it rolling at the Intelligentsia Cup, the Chris Thater Memorial, and other NCC races.

Aitcheson won two races in Illinois, the Glencoe Grand Prix and the Cobb Park Criterium in Kankakee. He won at Glencoe after lapping the field with Gateway Harley-Davidson's Bryan Gomez, and a former teammate from his Panther days, Ryan Knapp. He won at Kankakee almost by accident. He was giving a lead-out to Eamon, but when Eamon's chain fell off in the final 200 meters, Aitcheson sprinted for the win. Eamon finished in fourth.

The crit squad was having fun. Things were going well. They only hoped that Frey was close to finding a sponsor to keep them rolling in 2017.

FREY AND CURIN had a glimmer of hope when they met with Dennis Klumb, president and CEO of KS Energy Services, based in New Berlin, Wisconsin. A cyclist himself, and a long-time supporter of cycling through his sponsorship of a local club as well as a stage of the TOAD, Klumb was introduced to Frey by a friend of a friend who knew someone who knew someone else—the typical cycling connection.

Frey and Curin presented a sponsorship proposal to Klumb to represent KS Energy at pro races. Clearly, it would be an angel sponsorship; KS Energy builds energy infrastructure. They don't drum up a lot of business among the bike race crowd. Their sponsorship of a cycling club and TOAD was a way to give back to the community.

They agreed to sponsor the Astellas team for the Intelligentsia Cup races in Chicago in late July, with a tentative agreement to sponsor the team for the 2017 season. The news hit like a bolt of lightning.

Unfortunately, racing in KS Energy kits at the two-day Intelligensia Cup, the team didn't perform well. The first race at Lake Bluff was canceled due to severe storms, and the Goose Island race was dominated by United Healthcare. Monk sprinted for seventh place. Ian Keough was the next KS Energy–Astellas rider, in 43rd place. It wasn't how they had hoped to perform for their new sponsor.

A month later, KS Energy made it clear that they would be unwilling to fund the full amount that the team needed for another season of racing, but they agreed to play a supporting role to a larger title sponsor if one could be found.

The team's final weekend of racing was the TD Bank Mayor's Cup in Boston, the season finale of the NRC series. Monk placed fifth and Aitcheson finished in 11th, and with that, the team was officially defunct, so they packed up their equipment while the awards ceremony was taking place a few blocks away. As the top three finishers poured champagne on each other's heads, the former Astellas guys emptied their water bottles into the gutter.

The party was officially over. Within hours, the Red Army would disband and disappear into the relative obscurity of cycling history.

There was much to be sad about after five years of bike racing. There would be no more lead-outs on the last lap or cross-country drives in the overloaded van. No more standing in the street photographing a teammate as he stands on the podium for the awards ceremony. Not in these kits. Not with these same guys. They would scatter to the four winds as soon as they left the race site. Some would drive home. Some would fly. Different flights. Different destinations.

That's how bike racing works. Riders band together with veritable strangers of similar talents for a given amount of time, become close like brothers and sisters by busting their butts for each other in the hope that one of them—it doesn't matter who—ends up on the podium. Then they load up the van and go to the next town to try it again. For a few years they wear the same jersey. Some of them go on to wear a different jersey. But they remain friends.

Every once in a while, riders will happen into something truly good. Something special that they wish could last forever. The right combination of people. The right set of circumstances. Good chemistry with good guys who know how to work together and win together. And then the moment is gone, and they can only hope to re-create it on the next team they ride for. It's a fleeting gift.

CHAPTER 19

CLOSING UP SHOP

Late in the 2016 season, Curin and Frey realized that the cavalry wasn't coming.

Astellas corporate issued a cease-and-desist order to stop the team from using its logo. After riding as the KS Energy team at Intelligentsia Cup in late July, they had become the Cycling Development Foundation Cycling Team. By then, the only riders still active were the crit squad members wearing the black-and-red kits from Specialized.

In the desperate hunt for a new title sponsor, there were brief moments of hope sparked by a promising conversation, an insider tip, or a timely introduction. But every good phone call was followed by a disappointing one. It was a familiar story, starting with a someone knows someone who knows someone else who can get a meeting with the right person at MegaCorp. And, time and time again, Frey had to chase the rabbit down the hole until it disappeared.

Curin and Frey felt they had proven that they were fully capable of running a team and could keep it going if they could just connect with the right sponsor. They had the machinery and personnel in place to field a team that could contend in any race they entered; they just needed cash. And it wasn't coming.

For much of the year, the primary objective was to pay their bills, even if it meant dipping into their personal savings. Cycling has enough horror stories of teams falling deeply in debt and riders not getting paid. If there was any hope of managing a team again in the future, they had to continue to keep their heads above water.

Managing a cycling team was more than a hobby for Curin and Frey. Committed to finding a way to keep the team afloat, they explored every opportunity with a full-on assault. Many sleepless nights were spent thinking of new ways to pitch the team.

The time to close up shop and sell off the remaining equipment was fast approaching. At the end of the season they surveyed their assets to determine what was left: a few spare bikes, two sprinter vans, and a bunch of odds and ends. Some bikes had been pilfered for replacement parts, so they would be difficult to sell. The wheels needed to be shipped back to Fast Forward per their contract. Other pieces could be sold anytime, and easily purchased again if a sponsor was found. Selling the vans, however, felt like throwing in the towel. And while it would erase some of their personal debt, it represented a definitive ending point that they weren't quite ready to accept.

Any amount was workable in their eyes, even if they had to limit the team to the minimum of eight riders. They knew how to do a lot with a little.

But even a little never came.

A month after the riders said their goodbyes in Boston, the final death knell was ringing in Chicago and Milwaukee. While awaiting a response from one last long shot at sponsorship, they missed the UCI registration deadline for the 2017 season. It was the end of the road.

As the reality sank in, there was a mix of relief and disappointment. And some bitterness. Frey was relieved at not having to manage every detail pertaining to 16 bike racers. He no longer had to schedule flights for eight riders living in six cities to arrive at a separate airport all within an hour of each other. Or ship a box of replacement wheels to a rider and hope that it reached him before the next race. That part was freeing.

They were also free from risk. Even though every rider accepted the risks inherent in bike racing, Curin and Frey felt personally responsible for putting 16 riders on the road where even a moment's inattentiveness could have catastrophic consequences. With the countless miles of flying, driving, and racing, something could go wrong on any given day. Receiving the call after a crash like the one in Gila or Green's accident sent a chill down their spines. Every time a rider broke a collarbone, Curin and Frey felt it.

They wouldn't miss the stress of dealing with riders who felt they deserved a larger role. Unhappy with how things were going, these riders would lash out at Frey and demand more love.

Every sports team in existence is prone to these tantrums. At various times, every rider has different ideas of how the team should be run or how responsibilities should be assigned in a race. If Frey did this . . . If Curin did that . . . If we went here . . . If we had done this . . . If they had worked for me there . . . In idle moments, any employee of any organization can solve all the world's problems and offer up solutions to every situation. Cyclists are no different. When the tension boiled over, riders retreated to neutral corners to wait for the anger to pass, or they simply stopped racing altogether.

Curin had endured his share of phone calls from angry people in the industry promising to retaliate against his team for doing something they didn't agree with. It wasn't a regular occurrence, but they were memorable. And some stuck in his craw.

Frey would hear of comments from outsiders about how his team should be run. He would hear it directly from other team directors like the one who offered to take over, or he would hear it secondhand from odd sources. Everyone has a better idea.

Generally, almost everyone associated with the team credited Frey and Curin for being forthright and honest in their dealings. The riders recognized how much heart the pair put into the team. They never promised more than they could deliver. They never pretended to be more than they really were. Each year, the riders knew, going in, what the team was going to be.

Not every team can make that claim.

The fact that the duo never stumbled into a boxcar full of money kept the team's growth rate slow and steady. The steps they made from one year to the next were about the right size.

The real disappointment in the withdrawal of Astellas's sponsorship was the lost momentum, not being able to make good on all the lessons they had learned. The 2015 season had felt almost like a graduation ceremony. And 2016's win at Athens Twilight was proof that they had truly earned their degree. So now, with a Doctorate in Bike Race Team Management and no team to manage, they felt like they were back to bagging groceries. At one time their long-term plan of gaining entry into the Amgen Tour and adding a women's team was only a season away. Now it felt like a century.

The bitterness was aimed at no one in particular. Perhaps it was aimed at the sport in general for being such a difficult lover.

At some point, though, there was positive reflection on the decisions and choices they had made and events that simply transpired. Like hiring Myerson, who brought the team to a new level of racing. Or that the team itself became more than just a group of guys racing their bikes; they were an extended family with a special connection that transcended the lifespan of the team.

But the frustration of not being able to find a sponsor can creep back in, and at some point, one has to ask, what's the point? Why did Curin bother to extend himself so far emotionally and professionally in a sport that is built on such a thin premise? Why did Frey take on such a time-consuming and energy-draining project that created stress and anxiety?

Tougher questions they ask from time to time are, "What did we accomplish? Was it worth it?"

If financial reward is the only measure, then no, the result was a dismal failure. Curin and Frey lost money in the deal. And those who didn't lose money made, when calculated out to an hourly rate, about $1.30 per hour before taxes.

That's fine; it was never intended to be a money-making venture for anyone. It would break even at best. It was a selfless act by two people who truly love a sport and wanted to contribute to it with no expectation of remuneration. Like the parents who step in and coach a Little League team when the regular coach retires, they did it because the baton was lying on the ground and they felt it needed to be picked up and carried forward for the good of their community. To enrich the lives of others.

That's good enough.

More people should try it.

CHAPTER 20

THE TAKING OF FUZHOU

Ryan Aitcheson's phone rang in mid-October.

"Want to go to China?"

Frey frequently started phone conversations with a non sequitur. It was his way of establishing the fact that he was going to talk about something that hadn't been discussed previously.

"China? What's in China?"

The Chinese government had been dumping large amounts of money into various sports ever since the 2008 Beijing Olympics, and the UCI had been working to improve the Asia Tour, so there were a number of week-long UCI stage races taking place in China.

The organizers of one such tour, the Tour of Fuzhou, were inviting the Astellas team to come and race their event in the middle of November, just four weeks away. Since the team was still listed in the UCI files as an active team for 2016, they were eligible to race through the end of the year, but not obligated.

Frey could have said no.

The race organizers said they would pay the team $8,000.

Frey said yes.

His first task would be to find six riders who would agree to go, not an easy task since the season had ended weeks prior. He would need to find six guys willing to get back on the bike and train for a UCI 2.2 stage race against teams from Australia, Africa, Iran, Japan, and other countries who were actively racing, unlike American teams who had hung their bikes on hooks for the past month.

The Tour of Fuzhou was the kind of race that was right in the road squad's wheelhouse. The five-day stage race was held in the mountainous Fujian province and featured four long road races, the kind that the road crew would thrive on. Conversely, the crit squad hadn't been on a ride longer than 60 miles since the Fort McClellan Road Race in April, and they had raced flat criteriums all summer. None of them had done much riding since September.

After numerous phone calls and endless emails, Frey was able to convince six riders to race in China in November. Five came from the crit squad: Ryan Aitcheson, Matt Green, Clay Murfet, Brandon "Monk" Feehery, and Eamon Lucas. And Jake Sitler, who had joined the crit squad after the road squad fell apart mid-season. They were the only ones willing. With just three weeks to prepare for a mountainous stage race, they laughed at their prospects.

The attitude going into the event was similar to the attitude the team took to the world championship team time trial a year earlier: "What do we have to lose?" And if the team was founded on the notion of rider development, then any experience it could deliver was a positive experience, right up to the bitter end.

The team packed their bags.

THE SIX PIECED TOGETHER TIDBITS of information gleaned from their 2014 European vacation and then accepted the idea that they'd wing it the rest of the way. Mechanic Matt Kelley had the most experience traveling to China; he had raced cyclocross there on three occasions. His insight was invaluable, and he would be traveling with the team as their mechanic and food advisor, telling them what not to eat or drink.

Two weeks prior to departure, Green opted out. He had enrolled in classes in Milwaukee and couldn't really afford to take the time to train or make the trip. He wanted the opportunity to ride with the Red Army one last time, but he was also committed to his future with Tracy.

Since Jake had been assigned to the road squad and didn't own a Specialized-branded kit, the team had to ignore the cease-and-desist order that Astellas had issued earlier and wear the Astellas Red Army kits. They were still identified as Astellas Pro Cycling according to the UCI, and that's what the race organizers would be expecting.

Scrambling to get back into race shape, they joked with each other about who had the hairiest legs and who was going to get dropped on the first climb.

Bike-racer humor.

FROM THE MOMENT THE TEAM touched down in Fuzhou, they knew it was going to be a special trip. The hotel shuttle took much longer than scheduled as it navigated the scant remains of a road washed away by a typhoon a month earlier. Had this been a normal stateside race, the riders would have been freaking out about the long bumpy drive, not having enough to eat, and getting to the hotel at 3 a.m. after a 13-hour flight. Instead, they remained upbeat and carefree with absolutely no hang-ups.

With only one day to prepare equipment, get credentials, attend meetings, learn the routine, figure out their meals, and acclimate to the 13-hour time change, everyone lapsed into bike-race mode. Kelley worked hard to prep the bikes, Frey took care of the administrative work, and the riders went out on an exploratory shakedown ride in the surrounding area, where they received rock star treatment as foreigners in a strange land. Yongtai, a small city far off the beaten path, served as their base of operations. Clearly, the locals rarely, if ever, saw American tourists. Activity in the villages came to a halt when the team rolled through.

For guys who had been traveling around the United States all summer being yelled at by motorists, mocked, or completely ignored, the phenomenon of being celebrities (or, more accurately, oddities) took some getting used to. The villagers looked at the riders in wide-eyed wonder, smiled broadly, and took pictures of them as they passed.

THE RACE ORGANIZATION at the Asia Tour races operates a little differently than its American counterpart. In America, each team travels with one or two cars, a van full of equipment, and sometimes a team bus, and they transfer to the race site on their own schedule. By virtue of Fuzhou's remoteness, team vans and buses were unable to make the trip, so arrangements were made to transport 140 bikes and riders in a caravan of military-like cargo trucks and slightly out-of-date tour buses. Team managers were issued Audi A6s to drive to each race and were escorted by local police at roughly 180 kilometers per hour. Frey set aside his law-abiding principles during these transfers.

The first stage was held in downtown Fuzhou. The 110-mile course consisted of multiple laps on a flat 8-mile loop on a city boulevard, followed by a long, steep climb to a summit finish overlooking the smog-enshrouded city. Air quality was atrocious, and the riders felt its effects early on.

Right from the gun, riders attacked the peloton to avoid the sketchiness of first-race jitters. Not 500 meters into the race, race radio announced the first breakaway, and Eamon was in it. It only lasted a few seconds, but it was a good sign. Meanwhile, at the back of the bunch, riders were getting dropped in the first kilometer, indicating a wide disparity in the abilities within this field.

Pishgaman Giant, a UCI Continental team from Iran, was the heavily favored defending champion. They controlled things tightly on the circuits, allowing breakaways to go at their pleasure. Ryan, as he had all season, found himself in the longest breakaway of the day. But when things ramped up near the climb, the race came back together as the entire peloton streaked toward the base of the climb.

Once the road tilted up, the Pishgaman riders went to the front and rode a tempo that shredded the field. The pack of 140 riders exploded when it hit the climb. Sitler, normally the last man standing on tough courses, was the first Astellas rider dropped. Then Eamon. Then Ryan. Monk went into survival mode to prevent himself from blowing up on the climb. Clay was the foremost Astellas rider and fought to finish in 50th place. All five of them beat the time cutoff by several minutes. Not bad for a bunch of crit racers.

Meanwhile, the Pishgaman team rode away from everyone and finished with all six of their riders placing in the top eight. Breathtaking.

The next day, stage 2 was fairly flat and uneventful. A two-man breakaway, consisting of a Korean Olympian and a former WorldTour rider, snuck away 40 km into the 126 km race and stayed away to the end.

The Astellas riders handled the terrain well, but the speeds set by the Pishgaman team in the final 20 miles and an untimely flat tire for Ryan in the final 10 miles destroyed their ability to form their patented lead-out. Monk managed to finish in seventh place in the field sprint to get a top-10 finish. It was another positive sign that the team could be competitive in this field.

The unrelenting speed of Pishgaman, combined with their remarkable finish on stage 1, was beginning to raise eyebrows in the peloton. The Astellas riders were savvy enough to know what speeds are normal for a pack of this caliber, and the high speeds that were sustained throughout the 80-mile race were nothing short of amazing. But no one spoke of doping in the dining hall or on the bus. Open speculation puts riders on the defensive and creates tension in the field. The team tried to dismiss their own suspicions by reminding each other that they had never raced against any of these teams before; they could only do their best and hope that the system worked to identify dopers.

An amusement park called "Happy World" provided the backdrop for the start of stage 3. The course featured two difficult climbs on narrow roads and passed through miles of beautiful tea farms. The field broke in two on the first climb and riders in the second group worked feverishly to catch the lead group. Ryan, Clay, and Eamon found themselves to be among the strongest riders in the second group, but they weren't able to muster the horsepower to catch the lead group driven by the Pishgaman team. Jake, who had spent more time tending to the family store than training for this event, stopped midway up the first climb, crawled into the team car, and retired from the race. He immediately experienced the odd mix of relief and disappointment that riders feel when they abandon a race.

In the lead-up to the race, the guys had been having a lot of fun sandbagging about how little they were able to train. It's what bike racers do, and it was difficult to tell who was serious and who wasn't. They all had reasons to be out of race shape. Jake had been insisting all along that he wouldn't last long, but no one believed him because they knew him to be a constant joker and a natural athlete with no quit in him. As it turned out, he was right.

Monk, who had remained strangely silent during those sandbagging sessions, managed to stay with the lead group over the second climb. He used his instincts to stay in the top 20 during the final kilometers. A savvy sprinter, he read the body language of those around him to figure out who would contest the sprint. He did his best to stay with those candidates but got boxed in when riders on either side of him converged on him in the final 500 meters. He patiently waited for daylight to open up between them and bolted through to finish in third place, guaranteeing himself a spot on the podium.

The team was ecstatic. A third place finish in a stage made the entire trip a success.

Walking around with a trophy after a criterium in Athens, Georgia, will garner a few handshakes. Carrying a third-place trophy around in a Chinese city after this race garnered the adoration of hundreds of cycling fans who pulled on rider's arms and thrust cameras in faces to take selfies with the American team. The team that finished in third place—the team with the biggest smiles—was the center of attention. Well aware that this was their last race together, the guys milked it for all they could.

With two stages left to race, they rose above the devil-may-care confidence that had brought them this far. The fifth stage suited their style of racing. It was reasonably flat, and after a few days of racing their fitness was already improving. Quiet conversations about the possibility of making something happen in the final stage were under way. If all four riders could make it up the final climb on stage 4, they might be able to pull out a miracle.

Upon returning to the hotel, Frey and Kelley began foraging for race food. Unable to carry much over from the United States, and without the luxury of simply running to WalMart to buy more, they had been pilfering candy bars from the box lunches and begging other teams for extra Gatorade all week. They didn't have a cooler, so everything the team drank during the races was at room temperature. They were on their last water bottles, with just enough to get through the final two stages. Reaching the finish would entail leaning on the generosity of other teams.

Most of the course profile for the Queen Stage, stage 4 of the Tour of Fuzhou looked rather tame, followed by a nasty spike at the finish. The course was a simple out-and-back route, rolling along the beautiful Dazhang River and then heading uphill for the final 12 miles, taking the riders from 700 feet above sea level up to almost 3,000 feet. A criterium specialist's worst nightmare.

The single steep climb was the only thing standing between the Astellas team and a chance to race in stage 5 on Sunday. They only needed to get to the finish ahead of the cutoff time, approximately 20 minutes behind the stage winner.

Just 300 meters into the race, Eamon found himself in the breakaway with five others. The Pishgaman team, with their overall race leader, was tending to the front of the peloton and allowed the breakaway to enjoy its freedom. Any aggression in the race would take place on the steep climb to the finish line. Until then, no one seemed to care what happened. While Eamon had fun in the lead group, the other Astellas riders chilled in the peloton and saved their legs.

When the peloton reached the base of the climb, the Iranian team went to the front and shook up the race again, as they had done on stage 1. Popped off the back in the first mile, each Astellas rider settled into his rhythm and climbed within his own limits easily beating the time cut. Eamon, who had spent the entire day in the breakaway, suffered the most and finished just a few seconds ahead of elimination.

Knackered and hungry, the team piled into the team car and flew down the mountain in search of food. If they hoped to do anything positive in stage 5, their recovery would need to start immediately.

STAGE 5 WAS AS CLOSE to a criterium as the UCI produces, an 11-mile circuit race on a relatively flat course with a fair number of turns in the final 5 kilometers.

Midway through the race, a breakaway was allowed to form and establish a lead. When the gap grew to a minute, Eamon and Ryan talked about bridging across. Should they go? Shouldn't they? Is it coming back? Will it stay away? The debate went on for about five minutes before Eamon convinced Ryan to go with him. They shot out of the pack and across the gap to the four-rider breakaway. With one lap to go, the breakaway held onto a 1:15 lead. At 12 km to go, the lead decreased to 30 seconds. The peloton had the breakaway in their sights and was closing in.

Behind the wheel of the team car, Frey knew that this was the perfect scenario; if anyone in the field made an effort to bring back the breakaway, Clay and Monk were ready to roll out their well-rehearsed sprint. Meanwhile, up ahead, Ryan and Eamon were under no pressure to do any work because help was closing in from behind. The kilometers ticked by. The field grew closer and closer. The breakaway reached the final technical kilometers with a very small lead.

As is typical when a breakaway knows it's about to be caught, the attacks started coming. Eamon stayed in contact with each of them, but Ryan faltered. Having done much of the work to help the breakaway succeed, he was now falling into no-man's land between the breakaway and the field. With 3 kilometers to go, Eamon attacked the remnants of the breakaway. Some chased, but the rest were dropped and quickly gobbled up by the hard-charging field led by Pishgaman.

Eamon's attack wasn't the same last-ditch effort normally seen in stages of the Tour de France, where a desperate little-known rider makes a final dig to grab some TV time. It wasn't a decoy attack to set up a possible sprint. It also wasn't a rider making a bid to win the most aggressive rider jersey. This was the final statement from a team that would disband as soon as it crossed the line. In a desperate attempt to go out with a victory, the team put together one final attack.

Eamon was enjoying the feeling that every bike racer hopes to experience in a critical moment: no resistance from the pedals, just pure emotion and adrenalin. He had every intention of winning the stage.

"No one else in the picture" is how cyclists describe winning solo. Freewheeling down the finish straight, accompanied only by the TV motorcycle, Eamon won ahead of Wisdom-Hengxiang's Wang Meiyin of China (already signed by a WorldTour team for the 2017 season). He gave the crowd a long victory salute, beaming with confidence and shock. Clay and Monk caught up to Eamon 100 meters beyond the finish line and hoisted him on their shoulders. Ryan reached them moments after Clay and Monk realized that Eamon was too heavy.

Frey, Sitler, and Kelley were quickly on the scene to hug the winner.

The Pishgaman team managed to place five riders in the top seven places overall, and their 37-year-old leader won the yellow jersey. Their celebration took place a few yards away, garnering the crowd's attention. For the Astellas team, winning an international race on the last possible day was a thrilling finale.

The local media interviewed Eamon following the race. Even in the final moments, he told the gaggle of journalists that the team was available for sponsors.

There were no takers.

EPILOGUE

When the end finally came, everyone felt as if the circus had packed up its tents and left town. The riders, no longer bound contractually to the Cycling Development Foundation, were free to sort out their respective futures.

In 2017, Green and Aitcheson joined up with Paul Martin's First Internet Bank Domestic Elite team based in Indianapolis. It would be Green's first year as an amateur since 2007. He accepted that.

Despite his many podium appearances, Aitcheson regretted having never won a PRT or NCC race. He won the races that he expected to win and made a decent living at the Continental level. In addition to his 2016 salary, he received $11,000 in prize money after taxes and "splits," which means he had shared much more with his teammates. Unquestionably, he was one of Astellas Pro Cycling's most successful riders.

Monk, Eamon, Murfet, and Ilesic joined forces and found a handful of sponsors. Crit Life was a team of four riders that raced as many crits as they could get to and jumped into a few Red Hook races as well. Eamon later returned to Europe for the first time since his stint on the USAC National Team and earned a spot on the Conti-level Delta Cycling Rotterdam team.

Jake Sitler and Ansel Dickey remained in the pro ranks, joining the Boston-based CCB-Velotooler team as it made the jump from Domestic Elite to Pro Continental.

Jake Silverberg returned to Florida and rode for the IM-MegaCycle team before returning to the Conti level with 303 Project.

Dan Gardner, Olly Moors, and Brecht Dhaene (2014–2015) continued racing in Britain and Europe. Brecht eventually took a job as a corporate recruiter in Belgium and put his race bike away for good.

Cortlan Brown (2013–2015) joined up with Utah-based Canyon Bikes, a Domestic Elite team that later became a Pro Continental squad known as the Hangar 15 Cycling Team, and competed in the 2017 Larry H. Miller Tour of Utah.

Justin Williams (2013–2015) won more than 20 races for the Cylance team in 2017, including the Dana Point Grand Prix and the Super Prime on Downer Ave.

Hogan Sills and Jake Rytlewski teamed up again on the Bissell-ABG-Giant team in Indianapolis.

Peter Olejniczak returned to top form in 2017, winning the inaugural Detroit Cycling Championship for Borah Factory Racing.

David Williams, Johnathan Freter, Max Jenkins, and the rest of the team scattered and found jobs in the real world.

It came as no surprise that in January 2017, a couple of months after the Tour of Fuzhou, two riders from the Pishgaman Giant team tested positive for the use of banned substances. The entire team was barred from competition for doping violations.

MANY OF THE RIDERS and staff continue to stay in contact and celebrate each other's highs and lows. The same jokes that kept their spirits high at San Dimas and Speed Week continue to get laughs years later. The bond is a lasting one and possibly the best trophy the sport can produce.

Otherwise, there remains very little physical evidence that any of this actually took place. Yacht clubs have glass cases full of trophies and flags dating back to the 1800s. Boxing gyms celebrate their athletes with trophies and boxing match posters. Cycling is different.

There is a Bicycling Hall of Fame in Davis, California, but the Cycling Development Foundation's accomplishments are not enshrined there. Any oversized cardboard checks or leaders' jerseys that were won by the team ended up in a dumpster when the van was cleaned out. Bib numbers from important victories lost their value over time, and if they weren't tucked into the technical guide from the Cascade Classic and saved, they were thrown away.

The Astellas team experience included other victories to savor: being a positive role model to the young fans who asked for autographs after Aitcheson won the Athens Twilight, or befriending 14-year-old Alex in Wisconsin who raised $500 to give away his own personal crowd prime so that he could participate despite being bound to a wheelchair. There was always the hope that an interaction with a young fan might spark greatness down the road.

For Curin and Frey, the victory was in providing a lot of riders with the opportunity to gain plenty of race experience and explore their full potential. They were also proud to see Hyde and Myerson win a cyclo-cross national championship in their respective categories in 2017 and 2018, knowing that they played a role in that achievement. Watching Brecht advance to the PCT level with the popular Wanty–Group Gobert team was certainly rewarding. The team managers count it as a win when a talented kid like Gardner is picked up by Sean Kelly's An Post team, and they can say, "I gave that guy half of my Chipotle burrito once!"

(Of course, they wouldn't have said that. Every bike racer knows that you get more food at Chipotle if you order the bowl, not the burrito.)

"THE SPORT IS DEAD." Industry insiders say this almost every. Single. Day. Especially after a good team goes under or a major event falls off the calendar. And everyone has their own idea of how to save the sport, but no one seems to know how to begin putting thoughts into action.

There is a sense that the sport is flawed and therefore impossible to correct. And a belief that it could be so much better if we did A instead of B. Or that USAC could be doing more, UCI needs to change something, Sponsor X needs to do that, Event Z could be promoted better if they did such and such, or Team Y should be run differently.

There is a tendency among people in the cycling industry to view things with a jaundiced eye, cynical and embittered. Perhaps it comes from continually playing the role of a jilted lover so many times, being drawn in by the true love of bike racing only to be pushed away by fickle sponsors.

"Here I am . . . at yet another damn bike race," they say every weekend, as if they had no say in the matter and no better option.

"I hate Interbike. It's my 25th trip," they say of the annual trade show that no one seems to enjoy, yet they keep returning.

"Another sponsor has pulled out," they say with despair.

There are negative aspects to a sport that struggles to become mainstream, and it's easy to get caught up in them. Those who are in the sport see the potential and feel frustrated when that potential isn't fully realized. There's nothing that an infusion of cash couldn't fix, yet the sport ambles along relying on a shaky revenue stream.

That cycling has embraced the fallacy of sponsorship is easy to understand. It appears to work at the Tour de France and other World-Tour events, so it's easy to assume that it should work everywhere, all the way down to the Category V amateur racer. But it doesn't, and something needs to change.

Other niche sports and activities thrive without sponsors. Many exist at an acceptable level with the outside hope that they may someday become more mainstream and enjoy an influx of money and popularity. Until those sponsors come knocking, they rely on different funding mechanisms.

Oddly enough, the little-known summertime activity of competitive drum and bugle corps has some interesting parallels to cycling:

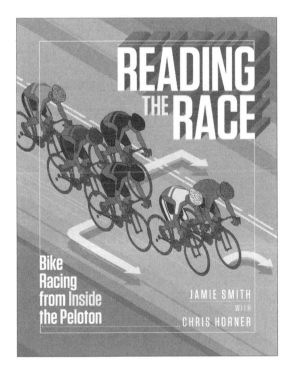

Competing corps traverse the country at enormous expense to perform before crowds of wildly enthusiastic followers from June to August. Participants live a monklike existence as they train long hours for 11-minute performances. They endure long bus rides and extended time away from their families in order to pursue their passion. And, just like cycling, it's an activity that the outside world doesn't really understand.

The glaring difference is that the top drum corps have operating budgets of $2 million with no reliance upon financial sponsors whatsoever. The smaller corps have budgets more than triple that of the Astellas team. Granted, tickets are sold at each of their performances, but gate receipts make up only a portion of their annual budget. The larger portion comes from donations as well as grassroots fundraising such as bingo, casino nights, and souvenir sales. They recruit dedicated volunteers to run their fundraising programs.

It takes a full-time effort to fulfill the budget requirements, but the model is sustainable, free from the woes of fleeting sponsorships, and focused on building up a dedicated fan base. The Vanguard Drum and Bugle Corps from Santa Clara, California, has been active for 50 years. Like the Astellas team, it is a development organization. Many of their alumni have gone on to become professional musicians and educators.

This model, or something like it, is a better plan for cycling at the Pro Continental level and below, where limited exposure fails to retain sponsors. But it requires an all-hands-on-deck attitude, which is lacking in cycling. As one Astellas rider remarked at the notion of fundraising, "That sounds like too much work. I'd rather just have a rich person write us a big check."

And there's the rub. It's a sentiment that's been pervasive throughout the sport for many years. We call it sponsorship, but it's often a quest for one generous donor.

Until a new mechanism is found, the sponsorship road will continue to be hard on its travelers. Frey and Curin had no choice but to take the hard road. It was the model available to them. Had they done nothing at all, their lives would have been much easier, but there would have been one less team on the road and 16 riders out of work.

The same can be said for the army of race promoters who, rather than just fretting about the state of the sport and about how many races have gone away, knowingly take the hard route and organize their bike races. They make mistakes and do things that aren't met with 100 percent approval.

But without directors and promoters, there is no sport. They get to do it their way because they're the ones actually doing it.

The sport is not dead. Far from it. A crop of young talented American riders have climbed their way onto the WorldTour and Pro Continental teams, with more promising young riders coming up through the ranks behind them. Continental teams such as Rally and Hincapie Racing have stepped up to the Pro Conti level, and new teams have entered at the Continental level to replace them. New events are in the planning stages in towns we don't yet know about. More will come and others will leave, while many will remain on the calendar.

As long as there are people willing to step into the void of leadership to contribute, the sport will continue to flourish. There's no barrier to entry. It just takes gumption.

Frey and Curin contributed to the betterment of the sport by playing an active role in it and by helping the next generation of pro racers find their way. They held up their pole in cycling's circus tent. That's how the sport works. It's not a Barnum or a Bailey who will reach down and to prop the tent up from above; it's the many workers who roll up their sleeves, grab a pole, and hold on tight while the performers put on a show for the public.

ABOUT THE AUTHOR

Jamie Smith is author of *Roadie: The Misunder-stood World of a Bike Racer* (winner of the 2009 Michigan Notable Book Award) and *Reading the Race: Bike Racing from Inside the Peloton*. He was a spin doctor for a nondescript suburb of Detroit for more than 25 years, writing speeches and press releases for the sleepy community. (His press releases were not what made the town sleepy.) Prior to working as a race announcer and soigneur, he held a variety of jobs that helped him prepare for a career in the cycling industry: marching band instructor, MLB scoreboard operator, gravedigger, and military policeman. He rode in his first bike race in 1982 and swore he had ridden his last race in 1997. And again in 2004 . . . and in 2012. He's a member of the Wolverine Sports Club. He lives somewhere in Michigan, where he races sailboats and cross-country skis.